A Wrinkle in Time

and Related Readings

McDougal Littell
A HOUGHTON MIFFLIN COMPANY
Evanston, Illinois   Boston   Dallas

Acknowledgments

Joanna Lewis Cole, Literary Agent for Judith Gorog: "Odd Jobs," from *A Taste for Quiet and Other Disquieting Tales* by Judith Gorog, copyright © 1982 by Judith Gorog. Reprinted by permission of Joanna Lewis Cole, Literary Agent.

New Directions Publishing Corporation: "Reversible," from *Collected Poems 1957–1987* by Octavio Paz in Spanish and English. Copyright © 1986 by Octavio Paz and Eliot Weinberger. Reprinted by permission of New Directions Publishing Corp.

William Morrow and Company: Excerpt from *World of the Brain* by Alvin and Virginia Silverstein. Copyright © 1986 by Alvin and Virginia Silverstein. By permission of William Morrow and Company.

Little, Brown and Company: "Andrew Holleman," from *It's Our World, Too!* by Phillip Hoose. Copyright © 1993 by Phillip Hoose. By permission of Little, Brown and Company.

Richard Kennedy: "The Dark Princess," from *Richard Kennedy: Collected Stories* by Richard Kennedy. Copyright © 1978 Richard Kennedy. By permission of the author.

The editors have made every effort to trace the ownership of all copyrighted selections in this book and to make full acknowledgement for their use. Omissions brought to our attention will be corrected in a subsequent edition.

A Wrinkle in Time by Madeleine L'Engle. Copyright © 1962 by Crosswicks, Ltd. All rights reserved. Copyright renewed © 1990 by Crosswicks, Ltd. Reprinted by arrangement with Farrar, Straus & Giroux, Inc.

Cover illustration by Ruben Ramos.
Author photo: Copyright © 1987 Amanda Smith.

ISBN 0-395-77154-4

567—DCI—02 01 00 99 98

Contents

Continued

A Wrinkle in Time

Madeleine L'Engle

Chapter 1

MRS. WHATSIT

It was a dark and stormy night.

In her attic bedroom Margaret Murry, wrapped in an old patchwork quilt, sat on the foot of her bed and watched the trees tossing in the frenzied lashing of the wind. Behind the trees clouds scudded frantically across the sky. Every few moments the moon ripped through them, creating wraithlike shadows that raced along the ground.

The house shook.

Wrapped in her quilt, Meg shook.

She wasn't usually afraid of weather. —It's not just the weather, she thought. —It's the weather on top of everything else. On top of me. On top of Meg Murry doing everything wrong.

School. School was all wrong. She'd been dropped down to the lowest section in her grade. That morning one of her teachers had said crossly, "Really, Meg, I don't understand how a child with parents as brilliant as yours are supposed to be can be such a poor student. If you don't manage to do a little better you'll have to stay back next year."

During lunch she'd rough-housed a little to try to make herself feel better, and one of the girls said scornfully, "After all, Meg, we aren't grammar-school kids any more. Why do you always act like such a baby?"

And on the way home from school, walking up the road with her arms full of books, one of the boys had said something about her "dumb baby brother." At this she'd thrown the books on the side of the road and tackled him with every ounce of strength she had, and arrived home with her blouse torn and a big bruise under one eye.

Sandy and Dennys, her ten-year-old twin brothers, who got home from school an hour earlier than she did, were disgusted. "Let *us* do the fighting when it's necessary," they told her.

—A delinquent, that's what I am, she thought grimly. —That's what they'll be saying next. Not Mother. But Them. Everybody Else. I wish Father—

But it was still not possible to think about her father without the danger of tears. Only her mother could talk about him in a natural way, saying, "When your father gets back—"

Gets back from where? And when? Surely her mother must know what people were saying, must be aware of the smugly vicious gossip. Surely it must hurt her as it did Meg. But if it did she gave no outward sign. Nothing ruffled the serenity of her expression.

—Why can't I hide it, too? Meg thought. Why do I always have to *show* everything?

The window rattled madly in the wind, and she pulled the quilt close about her. Curled up on one of her pillows a gray fluff of kitten yawned, showing its pink tongue, tucked its head under again, and went back to sleep.

Everybody was asleep. Everybody except Meg.

Even Charles Wallace, the "dumb baby brother," who had an uncanny way of knowing when she was awake and unhappy, and who would come, so many nights, tiptoeing up the attic stairs to her—even Charles Wallace was asleep.

How could they sleep? All day on the radio there had been hurricane warnings. How could they leave her up in the attic in the rickety brass bed, knowing that the roof might be blown right off the house, and she tossed out into the wild night sky to land who knows where?

Her shivering grew uncontrollable.

—You asked to have the attic bedroom, she told herself savagely. —Mother let you have it because you're the oldest. It's a privilege, not a punishment.

"Not during a hurricane, it isn't a privilege," she said aloud. She tossed the quilt down on the foot of the bed, and stood up. The kitten stretched luxuriously, and looked up at her with huge, innocent eyes.

"Go back to sleep," Meg said. "Just be glad you're a kitten and not a monster like me." She looked at herself in the wardrobe mirror and made a horrible face, baring a mouthful of teeth covered with braces. Automatically she pushed her glasses into position, ran her fingers through her mouse-brown hair, so that it stood wildly on end, and let out a sigh almost as noisy as the wind.

The wide wooden floorboards were cold against her feet. Wind blew in the crevices about the window frame, in spite of the protection the storm sash was supposed to offer. She could hear wind howling in the chimneys. From all the way downstairs she could hear Fortinbras, the big black dog, starting to bark. He must be frightened, too. What was he barking at? Fortinbras never barked without reason.

Suddenly she remembered that when she had gone to the post office to pick up the mail she'd heard about a tramp who was supposed to have stolen twelve sheets from Mrs. Buncombe, the constable's wife. They hadn't caught him, and maybe he was heading for the Murrys' house right now, isolated on a back road as it was; and this time maybe he'd be after more than sheets. Meg hadn't paid much attention to the talk about the tramp at the time, because the postmistress, with a sugary smile, had asked if she'd heard from her father lately.

She left her little room and made her way through the shadows of the main attic, bumping against the ping-pong table. —Now I'll have a bruise on my hip on top of everything else, she thought.

Next she walked into her old dolls' house, Charles Wallace's rocking horse, the twins' electric trains. "Why must everything happen to me?" She demanded of a large teddy bear.

At the foot of the attic stairs she stood still and listened. Not a sound from Charles Wallace's room on the right. On the left, in her parents' room, not a rustle from her mother sleeping alone in the great double bed. She tiptoed down the hall and into the twins' room, pushing again at her glasses as though they could help her to see better in the dark. Dennys was snoring. Sandy murmured something about baseball and subsided. The twins didn't have any problems. They weren't great students, but they weren't bad ones, either. They were perfectly content with a succession of B's and an occasional A or C. They were strong and fast runners and good at games, and when cracks were made about anybody in the Murry family, they weren't made about Sandy and Dennys.

She left the twins' room and went on downstairs,

avoiding the creaking seventh step. Fortinbras had stopped barking. It wasn't the tramp this time, then. Fort would go on barking if anybody was around.

—But suppose the tramp *does* come? Suppose he has a knife? Nobody lives near enough to hear if we screamed and screamed and screamed. Nobody'd care, anyhow. —I'll make myself some cocoa, she decided. —That'll cheer me up, and if the roof blows off at least I won't go off with it.

In the kitchen a light was already on, and Charles Wallace was sitting at the table drinking milk and eating bread and jam. He looked very small and vulnerable sitting there alone in the big old-fashioned kitchen, a blond little boy in faded blue Dr. Dentons, his feet swinging a good six inches above the floor.

"Hi," he said cheerfully. "I've been waiting for you."

From under the table where he was lying at Charles Wallace's feet, hoping for a crumb or two, Fortinbras raised his slender dark head in greeting to Meg, and his tail thumped against the floor. Fortinbras had arrived on their doorstep, a half-grown puppy, scrawny and abandoned, one winter night. He was, Meg's father had decided, part Llewellyn setter and part greyhound, and he had a slender, dark beauty that was all his own.

"Why didn't you come up to the attic?" Meg asked her brother, speaking as though he were at least her own age. "I've been scared stiff."

"Too windy up in that attic of yours," the little boy said. "I knew you'd be down. I put some milk on the stove for you. It ought to be hot by now."

How did Charles Wallace always know about her? How could he always tell? He never knew—or seemed to care—what Dennys or Sandy were thinking. It was his mother's mind, and Meg's, that he probed with frightening accuracy.

Was it because people were a little afraid of him that they whispered about the Murrys' youngest child, who was rumored to be not quite bright? "I've heard that clever people often have subnormal children," Meg had once overheard. "The two boys seem to be nice, regular children, but that unattractive girl and the baby boy certainly aren't all there."

It was true that Charles Wallace seldom spoke when anybody was around, so that many people thought he'd never learned to talk. And it was true that he hadn't talked at all until he was almost four. Meg would turn white with fury when people looked at him and clucked, shaking their heads sadly.

"Don't worry about Charles Wallace, Meg," her father had once told her. Meg remembered it very clearly because it was shortly before he went away. "There's nothing the matter with his mind. He just does things in his own way and in his own time."

"I don't want him to grow up to be dumb like me," Meg had said.

"Oh, my darling, you're not dumb," her father answered. "You're like Charles Wallace. Your development has to go at its own pace. It just doesn't happen to be the usual pace."

"How do you *know?*" Meg had demanded. "How do you *know* I'm not dumb? Isn't it just because you love me?"

"I love you, but that's not what tells me. Mother and I've given you a number of tests, you know."

Yes, that was true. Meg had realized that some of the "games" her parents played with her were tests of some kind, and that there had been more for her and Charles Wallace than for the twins. "IQ tests, you mean?"

"Yes, some of them."

"Is my IQ okay?"

"More than okay."

"What is it?"

"That I'm not going to tell you. But it assures me that both you and Charles Wallace will be able to do pretty much whatever you like when you grow up to yourselves. You just wait till Charles Wallace starts to talk. You'll see."

How right he had been about that, though he himself had left before Charles Wallace began to speak, suddenly, with none of the usual baby preliminaries, using entire sentences. How proud he would have been!

"You'd better check the milk," Charles Wallace said to Meg now, his diction clearer and cleaner than that of most five-year-olds. "You know you don't like it when it gets a skin on top."

"You put in more than twice enough milk." Meg peered into the saucepan.

Charles Wallace nodded serenely. "I thought Mother might like some."

"I might like what?" a voice said, and there was their mother standing in the doorway.

"Cocoa," Charles Wallace said. "Would you like a liverwurst-and-cream-cheese sandwich? I'll be happy to make you one."

"That would be lovely," Mrs. Murry said, "but I can make it myself if you're busy."

"No trouble at all." Charles Wallace slid down from his chair and trotted over to the refrigerator, his pajamaed feet padding softly as a kitten's. "How about you, Meg?" he asked. "Sandwich?"

"Yes, please," she said. "But not liverwurst. Do we have any tomatoes?"

Charles Wallace peered into the crisper. "One. All right if I use it on Meg, Mother?"

"To what better use could it be put?" Mrs. Murry smiled. "But not so loud, please, Charles. That is, unless you want the twins downstairs, too."

"Let's be exclusive," Charles Wallace said. "That's my new word for the day. Impressive, isn't it?"

"Prodigious," Mrs. Murry said. "Meg, come let me look at that bruise."

Meg knelt at her mother's feet. The warmth and light of the kitchen had relaxed her so that her attic fears were gone. The cocoa steamed fragrantly in the saucepan; geraniums bloomed on the window sills and there was a bouquet of tiny yellow chrysanthemums in the center of the table. The curtains, red, with a blue and green geometrical pattern, were drawn, and seemed to reflect their cheerfulness throughout the room. The furnace purred like a great, sleepy animal; the lights glowed with steady radiance; outside, alone in the dark, the wind still battered against the house, but the angry power that had frightened Meg while she was alone in the attic was subdued by the familiar comfort of the kitchen. Underneath Mrs. Murry's chair Fortinbras let out a contented sigh.

Mrs. Murry gently touched Meg's bruised cheek. Meg looked up at her mother, half in loving admiration, half in sullen resentment. It was not an advantage to have a mother who was a scientist and a beauty as well. Mrs. Murry's flaming red hair, creamy skin, and violet eyes with long dark lashes, seemed even more spectacular in comparison with Meg's outrageous plainness. Meg's hair had been passable as long as she wore it tidily in braids. When she went into high school it was cut, and now she and her mother struggled with putting it up, but one side would come out curly and the other straight, so that she looked even plainer than before.

"You don't know the meaning of moderation, do you, my darling?" Mrs. Murry asked. "A happy medium is something I wonder if you'll ever learn. That's a nasty bruise the Henderson boy gave you. By the way, shortly after you'd gone to bed his mother called up to complain about how badly you'd hurt him. I told her that since he's a year older and at least twenty-five pounds heavier than you are, I thought I was the one who ought to be doing the complaining. But she seemed to think it was all your fault."

"I suppose that depends on how you look at it," Meg said. "Usually no matter what happens people think it's my fault, even if I have nothing to do with it at all. But I'm sorry I tried to fight him. It's just been an awful week. And I'm full of bad feeling."

Mrs. Murry stroked Meg's shaggy head. "Do you know why?"

"I *hate* being an oddball," Meg said. "It's hard on Sandy and Dennys, too. I don't know if they're really like everybody else, or if they're just able to pretend they are. I try to pretend, but it isn't any help."

"You're much too straightforward to be able to pretend to be what you aren't," Mrs. Murry said. "I'm sorry, Meglet. Maybe if Father were here he could help you, but I don't think I can do anything till you've managed to plow through some more time. Then things will be easier for you. But that isn't much help right now, is it?"

"Maybe if I weren't so repulsive-looking—maybe if I were pretty like you—"

"Mother's not a bit pretty; she's beautiful," Charles Wallace announced, slicing liverwurst. "Therefore I bet she was awful at your age."

"How right you are," Mrs. Murry said. "Just give yourself time, Meg."

"Lettuce on your sandwich, Mother?" Charles Wallace asked.

"No, thanks."

He cut the sandwich into sections, put it on a plate, and set it in front of his mother. "Yours'll be along in just a minute, Meg. I think I'll talk to Mrs. Whatsit about you."

"Who's Mrs. Whatsit?" Meg asked.

"I think I want to be exclusive about her for a while," Charles Wallace said. "Onion salt?"

"Yes, please."

"What's Mrs. Whatsit stand for?" Mrs. Murry asked.

"That's her name," Charles Wallace answered. "You know the old shingled house back in the woods that the kids won't go near because they say it's haunted? That's where they live."

"They?"

"Mrs. Whatsit and her two friends. I was out with Fortinbras a couple of days ago—you and the twins were at school, Meg. We like to walk in the woods, and suddenly he took off after a squirrel and I took off after him and we ended up by the haunted house, so I met them by accident, as you might say."

"But nobody lives there," Meg said.

"Mrs. Whatsit and her friends do. They're very enjoyable."

"Why didn't you tell me about it before?" Mrs. Murry asked. "And you know you're not supposed to go off our property without permission, Charles."

"I know," Charles said. "That's one reason I didn't tell you. I just rushed off after Fortinbras without thinking. And then I decided, well, I'd better save them for an emergency, anyhow."

A fresh gust of wind took the house and shook it, and suddenly the rain began to lash against the windows.

"I don't think I like this wind," Meg said nervously.

"We'll lose some shingles off the roof, that's certain," Mrs. Murry said. "But this house has stood for almost two hundred years and I think it will last a little longer, Meg. There's been many a high wind up on this hill."

"But this is a hurricane!" Meg wailed. "The radio kept saying it was a hurricane!"

"It's October," Mrs. Murry told her. "There've been storms in October before."

As Charles Wallace gave Meg her sandwich Fortinbras came out from under the table. He gave a long, low growl, and they could see the dark fur slowly rising on his back. Meg felt her own skin prickle.

"What's wrong?" she asked anxiously.

Fortinbras stared at the door that opened into Mrs. Murry's laboratory which was in the old stone dairy right off the kitchen. Beyond the lab a pantry led outdoors, though Mrs. Murry had done her best to train the family to come into the house through the garage door or the front door and not through her lab. But it was the lab door and not the garage door toward which Fortinbras was growling.

"You didn't leave any nasty-smelling chemicals cooking over a Bunsen burner, did you, Mother?" Charles Wallace asked.

Mrs. Murry stood up. "No. But I think I'd better go see what's upsetting Fort, anyhow."

"It's the tramp, I'm sure it's the tramp," Meg said nervously.

"What tramp?" Charles Wallace asked.

"They were saying at the post office this afternoon that a tramp stole all Mrs. Buncombe's sheets."

"We'd better sit on the pillow cases, then," Mrs.

Murry said lightly. "I don't think even a tramp would be out on a night like this, Meg."

"But that's probably why he *is* out," Meg wailed, "trying to find a place *not* to be out."

"In which case I'll offer him the barn till morning." Mrs. Murry went briskly to the door.

"I'll go with you." Meg's voice was shrill.

"No, Meg, you stay with Charles and eat your sandwich."

"Eat!" Meg exclaimed as Mrs. Murry went out through the lab. "How does she expect me to eat?"

"Mother can take care of herself," Charles said. "Physically, that is." But he sat in his father's chair at the table and his legs kicked at the rungs; and Charles Wallace, unlike most small children, had the ability to sit still.

After a few moments that seemed like forever to Meg, Mrs. Murry came back in, holding the door open for—was it the tramp? It seemed small for Meg's idea of a tramp. The age or sex was impossible to tell, for it was completely bundled up in clothes. Several scarves of assorted colors were tied about the head, and a man's felt hat perched atop. A shocking pink stole was knotted about a rough overcoat, and black rubber boots covered the feet.

"Mrs. Whatsit," Charles said suspiciously, "what are you doing here? And at this time of night, too?"

"Now don't you be worried, my honey." A voice emerged from among turned-up coat collar, stole, scarves, and hat, a voice like an unoiled gate, but somehow not unpleasant.

"Mrs.—uh—Whatsit—says she lost her way," Mrs. Murry said. "Would you care for some hot chocolate, Mrs. Whatsit?"

"Charmed, I'm sure," Mrs. Whatsit answered, taking off the hat and the stole. "It isn't so much that

I lost my way as that I got blown off course. And when I realized that I was at little Charles Wallace's house I thought I'd just come in and rest a bit before proceeding on my way."

"How did you know this was Charles Wallace's house?" Meg asked.

"By the smell." Mrs. Whatsit untied a blue and green paisley scarf, a red and yellow flowered print, a gold Liberty print, a red and black bandanna. Under all this a sparse quantity of grayish hair was tied in a small but tidy knot on top of her head. Her eyes were bright, her nose a round, soft blob, her mouth puckered like an autumn apple. "My, but it's lovely and warm in here," she said.

"Do sit down." Mrs. Murry indicated a chair. "Would you like a sandwich, Mrs. Whatsit? I've had liverwurst and cream cheese; Charles has had bread and jam; and Meg, lettuce and tomato."

"Now, let me see," Mrs. Whatsit pondered. "I'm passionately fond of Russian caviar."

"You peeked!" Charles cried indignantly. "We're saving that for Mother's birthday and you can't have any!"

Mrs. Whatsit gave a deep and pathetic sigh.

"*No,*" Charles said. "Now, you mustn't give in to her, Mother, or I shall be very angry. How about tuna-fish salad?"

"All right," Mrs. Whatsit said meekly.

"I'll fix it," Meg offered, going to the pantry for a can of tuna fish.

—For crying out loud, she thought,—this old woman comes barging in on us in the middle of the night and Mother takes it as though there weren't anything peculiar about it at all. I'll bet she *is* the tramp. I'll bet she *did* steal those sheets. And she's certainly no one Charles Wallace ought to be friends with, especially when he won't even talk to ordinary people.

"I've only been in the neighborhood a short time," Mrs. Whatsit was saying as Meg switched off the pantry light and came back into the kitchen with the tuna fish, "and I didn't think I was going to like the neighbors at all until dear little Charles came over with his dog."

"Mrs. Whatsit," Charles Wallace demanded severely, "why did you take Mrs. Buncombe's sheets?"

"Well, I *needed* them, Charles dear."

"You must return them at once."

"But Charles, dear, I *can't*. I've *used* them."

"It was very wrong of you," Charles Wallace scolded. "If you needed sheets that badly you should have asked me."

Mrs. Whatsit shook her head and clucked. "You can't spare any sheets. Mrs. Buncombe can."

Meg cut up some celery and mixed it in with the tuna. After a moment's hesitation she opened the refrigerator door and brought out a jar of little sweet pickles. —Though why I'm doing it for her I don't know, she thought, as she cut them up. —I don't trust her one bit.

"Tell your sister I'm all right," Mrs. Whatsit said to Charles. "Tell her my intentions are good."

"The road to hell is paved with good intentions," Charles intoned.

"My, but isn't he cunning." Mrs. Whatsit beamed at him fondly. "It's lucky he has someone to understand him."

"But I'm afraid he doesn't," Mrs. Murry said. "None of us is quite up to Charles."

"But at least you aren't trying to squash him down." Mrs. Whatsit nodded her head vigorously. "You're letting him be himself."

"Here's your sandwich," Meg said, bringing it to Mrs. Whatsit.

"Do you mind if I take off my boots before I eat?" Mrs. Whatsit asked, picking up the sandwich nevertheless. "Listen." She moved her feet up and down in her boots, and they could hear water squelching. "My toes are ever so damp. The trouble is that these boots are a mite too tight for me, and I never can take them off by myself."

"I'll help you," Charles offered.

"Not you. You're not strong enough."

"I'll help." Mrs. Murry squatted at Mrs. Whatsit's feet, yanking on one slick boot. When the boot came off it came suddenly. Mrs. Murry sat down with a thump. Mrs. Whatsit went tumbling backward with the chair onto the floor, sandwich held high in one old claw. Water poured out of the boot and ran over the floor and the big braided rug.

"Oh, dearie me," Mrs. Whatsit said, lying on her back in the overturned chair, her feet in the air, one in a red and white striped sock, the other still booted.

Mrs. Murry got to her feet. "Are you all right, Mrs. Whatsit?"

"If you have some liniment I'll put it on my dignity," Mrs. Whatsit said, still supine. "I think it's sprained. A little oil of cloves mixed well with garlic is rather good." And she took a large bite of sandwich.

"Do please get up," Charles said. "I don't like to see you lying there that way. You're carrying things too far."

"Have you ever tried to get to your feet with a sprained dignity?" But Mrs. Whatsit scrambled up, righted the chair, and then sat back down on the floor, the booted foot stuck out in front of her, and took another bite. She moved with great agility for such an old woman. At least Meg was reasonably sure that she was an old woman, and a very old woman at that.

Mrs. Whatsit, her mouth full, ordered Mrs. Murry, "Now pull while I'm already down."

Quite calmly, as though this old woman and her boots were nothing out of the ordinary, Mrs. Murry pulled until the second boot relinquished the foot. This foot was covered with a blue and gray Argyle sock, and Mrs. Whatsit sat there, wriggling her toes, contentedly finishing her sandwich before scrambling to her feet. "Ah," she said, "that's ever so much better," and took both boots and shook them out over the sink. "My stomach is full and I'm warm inside and out and it's time I went home."

"Don't you think you'd better stay till morning?" Mrs. Murry asked.

"Oh, thank you, dearie, but there's *so* much to do I just can't waste time sitting around frivoling."

"It's much too wild a night to travel in."

"Wild nights are my glory," Mrs. Whatsit said. "I just got caught in a down draft and blown off course."

"Well, at least till your socks are dry—"

"Wet socks don't bother me. I just didn't like the water squishing around in my boots. Now don't worry about me, lamb." (Lamb was not a word one would ordinarily think of calling Mrs. Murry.) "I shall just sit down for a moment and pop on my boots and then I'll be on my way. Speaking of ways, pet, by the way, there *is* such a thing as a tesseract."

Mrs. Murry went very white and with one hand reached backward and clutched at a chair for support. Her voice trembled. "What did you say?"

Mrs. Whatsit tugged at her second boot. "I said," she grunted, shoving her foot down in, "that there is"—shove—"such a thing"—shove—"as a tesseract." Her foot went down into the boot, and grabbing shawls, scarves, and hat, she hustled out the door.

Mrs. Murry stayed very still, making no move to help the old woman. As the door opened, Fortinbras streaked in, panting, wet and shiny as a seal. He looked at Mrs. Murry and whined.

The door slammed.

"Mother, what's the matter!" Meg cried. "What did she say? What is it?"

"The tesseract—" Mrs. Murry whispered. "What did she mean? How could she have known?"

Chapter 2

MRS. WHO

When Meg woke to the jangling of her alarm clock the wind was still blowing but the sun was shining; the worst of the storm was over. She sat up in bed, shaking her head to clear it.

It must have been a dream. She'd been frightened by the storm and worried about the tramp so she'd just dreamed about going down to the kitchen and seeing Mrs. Whatsit and having her mother get all frightened and upset by that word—what was it? Tess—tess something.

She dressed hurriedly, picked up the kitten still curled up on the bed, and dumped it unceremoniously on the floor. The kitten yawned, stretched, gave a piteous miaow, trotted out of the attic and down the stairs. Meg made her bed and hurried after it. In the kitchen her mother was making French toast and the twins were already at the table. The kitten was lapping milk out of a saucer.

"Where's Charles?" Meg asked.

"Still asleep. We had rather an interrupted night, if you remember."

"I hoped it was a dream," Meg said.

Her mother carefully turned over four slices of French toast, then said in a steady voice, "No, Meg. Don't hope it was a dream. I don't understand it any more than you do, but one thing I've learned is that you don't have to understand things for them to *be.* I'm sorry I showed you I was upset. Your father and I used to have a joke about tesseract."

"What *is* a tesseract?" Meg asked.

"It's a concept." Mrs. Murry handed the twins the syrup. "I'll try to explain it to you later. There isn't time before school."

"I don't see why you didn't wake us up," Dennys said. "It's a gyp we missed out on all the fun."

"You'll be a lot more awake in school today than I will." Meg took her French toast to the table.

"Who cares," Sandy said. "If you're going to let old tramps come into the house in the middle of the night, Mother, you ought to have Den and me around to protect you."

"After all, Father would expect us to," Dennys added.

"We know you have a great mind and all, Mother," Sandy said, "but you don't have much *sense.* And certainly Meg and Charles don't."

"I know. We're morons." Meg was bitter.

"I wish you wouldn't be such a *dope,* Meg. Syrup, please." Sandy reached across the table. "You don't have to take everything so *per*sonally. Use a happy *medium,* for heaven's sake. You just goof around in school and look out the window and don't pay any attention."

"You just make things harder for yourself," Dennys said. "And Charles Wallace is going to have an awful time next year when he starts school. *We* know he's bright, but he's so funny when he's around other people and they're so used to thinking he's dumb, I don't know what's going to happen to him. Sandy and I'll sock anybody who picks on him, but that's about all we can do."

"Let's not worry about next year till we get through this one," Mrs. Murry said. "More French toast, boys?"

At school Meg was tired and her eyelids sagged and her mind wandered. In social studies she was asked to name the principal imports and exports of Nicaragua, and though she had looked them up dutifully the evening before, now she could remember none of them. The teacher was sarcastic, the rest of the class laughed, and she flung herself down in her seat in a fury. "Who *cares* about the imports and exports of Nicaragua, anyhow?" she muttered.

"If you're going to be rude, Margaret, you may leave the room," the teacher said.

"Okay, I will." Meg flounced out.

During study hall the principal sent for her. "What seems to be the problem now, Meg?" he asked, pleasantly enough.

Meg looked sulkily down at the floor. "Nothing, Mr. Jenkins."

"Miss Porter tells me you were inexcusably rude."

Meg shrugged.

"Don't you realize that you just make everything harder for yourself by your attitude?" the principal asked. "Now, Meg, *I'm* convinced that you can do the work and keep up with your grade if you will apply yourself, but some of your teachers are not. You're going to have to do something about yourself. Nobody can do it for you." Meg was silent. "Well? What about it, Meg?"

"I don't know what to do," Meg said.

"You could do your homework, for one thing. Wouldn't your mother help you?"

"If I asked her to."

"Meg, is something troubling you? Are you unhappy at home?" Mr. Jenkins asked.

At last Meg looked at him, pushing at her glasses in a characteristic gesture. "Everything's *fine* at home."

"I'm glad to hear it. But I know it must be hard on you to have your father away."

Meg eyed the principal warily, and ran her tongue over the barbed line of her braces.

"Have you had any news from him lately?"

Meg was sure it was not only imagination that made her feel that behind Mr. Jenkins' surface concern was a gleam of avid curiosity. Wouldn't he like to know! she thought. And if I knew anything he's the last person I'd tell. Well, one of the last.

The postmistress must know that it was almost a year now since the last letter, and heaven knows how many people *she'd* told, or what unkind guesses she'd made about the reason for the long silence.

Mr. Jenkins waited for an answer, but Meg only shrugged.

"Just what was your father's line of business?" Mr. Jenkins asked. "Some kind of scientist, wasn't he?"

"He *is* a physicist." Meg bared her teeth to reveal the two ferocious lines of braces.

"Meg, don't you think you'd make a better adjustment to life if you faced facts?"

"I do face facts," Meg said. "They're lots easier to face than people, I can tell you."

"Then why don't you face facts about your father?"

"You leave my father out of it!" Meg shouted.

"Stop bellowing," Mr. Jenkins said sharply. "Do you want the entire school to hear you?"

"So what?" Meg demanded. "I'm not ashamed of anything I'm saying. Are you?"

Mr. Jenkins sighed. "Do you enjoy being the most belligerent, uncooperative child in school?"

Meg ignored this. She leaned over the desk toward the principal. "Mr. Jenkins, you've met my mother, haven't you? You can't accuse her of not facing facts, can you? She's a scientist. She has doctors' degrees in both biology and bacteriology. Her *business* is facts. When she tells me that my father isn't coming home, I'll believe it. As long as she says Father *is* coming home, then I'll believe that."

Mr. Jenkins sighed again. "No doubt your mother wants to believe that your father is coming home, Meg. Very well, I can't do anything else with you. Go on back to study hall. Try to be a little less antagonistic. Maybe your work would improve if your general attitude were more tractable."

When Meg got home from school her mother was in the lab, the twins were at Little League, and Charles Wallace, the kitten, and Fortinbras were waiting for her. Fortinbras jumped up, put his front paws on her shoulders, and gave her a kiss, and the kitten rushed to his empty saucer and mewed loudly.

"Come on," Charles Wallace said. "Let's go."

"Where?" Meg asked. "I'm hungry, Charles. I don't want to go anywhere till I've had something to eat." She was still sore from the interview with Mr. Jenkins, and her voice sounded cross. Charles Wallace looked at her thoughtfully as she went to the refrigerator and gave the kitten some milk, then drank a mugful herself.

He handed her a paper bag. "Here's a sandwich

and some cookies and an apple. I thought we'd better go see Mrs. Whatsit."

"Oh, golly," Meg said. "*Why,* Charles?"

"You're still uneasy about her, aren't you?" Charles asked.

"Well, yes."

"Don't be. She's all right. I promise you. She's on our side."

"How do you know?"

"*Meg,*" he said impatiently. "I *know.*"

"But why should we go see her now?"

"I want to find out more about that tesseract thing. Didn't you see how it upset Mother? You know when Mother can't control the way she feels, when she lets us see she's upset, then it's something big."

Meg thought for a moment. "Okay, let's go. But let's take Fortinbras with us."

"Well, of course. He needs the exercise."

They set off, Fortinbras rushing ahead, then doubling back to the two children, then leaping off again. The Murrys lived about four miles out of the village. Behind the house was a pine woods and it was through this that Charles Wallace took Meg.

"Charles, you know she's going to get in awful trouble—Mrs. Whatsit, I mean—if they find out she's broken into the haunted house. And taking Mrs. Buncombe's sheets and everything. They could send her to jail."

"One of the reasons I want to go over this afternoon is to warn them."

"Them?"

"I told you she was there with her two friends. I'm not even sure it was Mrs. Whatsit herself who took the sheets, though I wouldn't put it past her."

"But what would she want all those sheets for?"

"I intend to ask her," Charles Wallace said, "and to tell them they'd better be more careful. I don't really think they'll let anybody find them, but I just thought we ought to mention the possibility. Sometime during vacations some of the boys go out there looking for thrills, but I don't think anybody's apt to right now, what with basketball and everything."

They walked in silence for a moment through the fragrant woods, the rusty pine needles gentle under their feet. Up above them the wind made music in the branches. Charles Wallace slipped his hand confidingly in Meg's, and the sweet, little-boy gesture warmed her so that she felt the tense knot inside her begin to loosen. *Charles* loves me at any rate, she thought.

"School awful again today?" he asked after a while.

"Yes. I got sent to Mr. Jenkins. He made snide remarks about Father."

Charles Wallace nodded sagely. "I know."

"*How* do you know?"

Charles Wallace shook his head. "I can't quite explain. You tell me, that's all."

"But I never say anything. You just seem to know."

"Everything about you tells me," Charles said.

"How about the twins?" Meg asked. "Do you know about them too?"

"I suppose I could if I wanted to. If they needed me. But it's sort of tiring, so I just concentrate on you and Mother."

"You mean you read our minds?"

Charles Wallace looked troubled. "I don't think it's that. It's being able to understand a sort of language, like sometimes if I concentrate very hard I can understand the wind talking with the trees. You tell me, you see, sort of inad—inadvertently. That's a good word, isn't it? I got Mother to look it up in the dictionary for me this morning. I really must learn to read, except I'm afraid it will make it awfully hard for me in school next year if I already know things. I think it will be better if people go on thinking I'm not very bright. They won't hate me quite so much."

Ahead of them Fortinbras started barking loudly, the warning bay that usually told them that a car was coming up the road or that someone was at the door.

"Somebody's here," Charles Wallace said sharply. "Somebody's hanging around the house. Come *on*." He started to run, his short legs straining. At the edge of the woods Fortinbras stood in front of a boy, barking furiously.

As they came panting up the boy said, "For crying out loud, call off your dog."

"Who is he?" Charles Wallace asked Meg.

"Calvin O'Keefe. He's in Regional, but he's older than I am. He's a big bug."

"It's all right, fella. I'm not going to hurt you," the boy said to Fortinbras.

"Sit, Fort," Charles Wallace commanded, and Fortinbras dropped to his haunches in front of the boy, a low growl still pulsing in his dark throat.

"Okay." Charles Wallace put his hands on his hips. "Now tell us what you're doing here."

"I might ask the same of you," the boy said with some indignation. "Aren't you two of the Murry kids? This isn't your property, is it?" He started to move, but Fortinbras' growl grew louder and he stopped.

"Tell me about him, Meg," Charles Wallace demanded.

"What would I know about him?" Meg asked.

"He's a couple of grades above me, and he's on the basketball team."

"Just because I'm tall." Calvin sounded a little embarrassed. Tall he certainly was, and skinny. His bony wrists stuck out of the sleeves of his blue sweater; his worn corduroy trousers were three inches too short. He had orange hair that needed cutting and the appropriate freckles to go with it. His eyes were an oddly bright blue.

"Tell us what you're doing here," Charles Wallace said.

"What *is* this? The third degree? Aren't you the one who's supposed to be the moron?"

Meg flushed with rage, but Charles Wallace answered placidly, "That's right. If you want me to call my dog off you'd better give."

"Most peculiar moron I've ever met," Calvin said. "I just came to get away from my family."

Charles Wallace nodded. "What kind of family?"

"They all have runny noses. I'm third from the top of eleven kids. I'm a sport."

At that Charles Wallace grinned widely. "So 'm I."

"I don't mean like in baseball," Calvin said.

"Neither do I."

"I mean like in biology," Calvin said suspiciously.

"*A change in gene,*" Charles Wallace quoted, "*resulting in the appearance in the offspring of a character which is not present in the parents but which is potentially transmissible to its offspring.*"

"What gives around here?" Calvin asked. "I was told you couldn't talk."

"Thinking I'm a moron gives people something to feel smug about," Charles Wallace said. "Why should I disillusion them? How old are you, Cal?"

"Fourteen."

"What grade?"

"Junior. Eleventh. I'm bright. Listen, did anybody ask you to come here this afternoon?"

Charles Wallace, holding Fort by the collar, looked at Calvin suspiciously. "What do you mean, *asked?*"

Calvin shrugged. "You still don't trust me, do you?"

"I don't *dis*trust you," Charles Wallace said.

"Do you want to tell me why you're here, then?"

"Fort and Meg and I decided to go for a walk. We often do in the afternoon."

Calvin dug his hands down in his pockets. "You're holding out on me."

"So're you," Charles Wallace said.

"Okay, old sport," Calvin said, "I'll tell you this much. Sometimes I get a feeling about things. You might call it a compulsion. Do you know what compulsion means?"

"*Constraint. Obligation. Because one is compelled.* Not a very good definition, but it's the Concise Oxford."

"Okay, okay," Calvin sighed. "I must remember I'm preconditioned in my concept of your mentality."

Meg sat down on the coarse grass at the edge of the woods. Fort gently twisted his collar out of Charles Wallace's hands and came over to Meg, lying down beside her and putting his head in her lap.

Calvin tried now politely to direct his words toward Meg as well as Charles Wallace, "When I get this feeling, this compulsion, I always do what it tells me. I can't explain where it comes from or how I get it, and it doesn't happen very often. But I obey it. And this afternoon I had a feeling that I must come over to the haunted house. That's all I know, kid. I'm not holding anything back. Maybe it's because I'm supposed to meet you. You tell *me.*"

Charles Wallace looked at Calvin probingly for a moment; then an almost glazed look came into his eyes, and he seemed to be thinking at him. Calvin stood very still, and waited.

At last Charles Wallace said. "Okay. I believe you. But I can't tell you. I think I'd like to trust you. Maybe you'd better come home with us and have dinner."

"Well, sure, but—what would your mother say to that?" Calvin asked.

"She'd be delighted. Mother's all right. She's not one of us. But she's all right."

"What about Meg?"

"Meg has it tough," Charles Wallace said. "She's not really one thing or the other."

"What do you mean, *one of us?*" Meg demanded. "What do you mean I'm not one thing or the other?"

"Not now, Meg," Charles Wallace said. "Slowly. I'll tell you about it later." He looked at Calvin, then seemed to make a quick decision. "Okay, let's take him to meet Mrs. Whatsit. If he's not okay she'll know." He started off on his short legs toward the dilapidated old house.

The haunted house was half in the shadows of the clump of elms in which it stood. The elms were almost bare, now, and the ground around the house was yellow with damp leaves. The late afternoon light had a greenish cast which the blank windows reflected in a sinister way. An unhinged shutter thumped. Something else creaked. Meg did not wonder that the house had a reputation for being haunted.

A board was nailed across the front door, but Charles Wallace led the way around to the back. The door there appeared to be nailed shut, too, but Charles Wallace knocked, and the door swung slowly outward, creaking on rusty hinges. Up in one of the elms an old black crow gave its raucous cry, and a woodpecker went into a wild ratatattat. A large gray rat scuttled around the corner of the house and Meg let out a stifled shriek.

"They get a lot of fun out of using all the typical props," Charles Wallace said in a reassuring voice. "Come on. Follow me."

Calvin put a strong hand to Meg's elbow, and Fort pressed against her leg. Happiness at their concern was so strong in her that her panic fled, and she followed Charles Wallace into the dark recesses of the house without fear.

They entered into a sort of kitchen. There was a huge fireplace with a big black pot hanging over a merry fire. Why had there been no smoke visible from the chimney? Something in the pot was bubbling, and it smelled more like one of Mrs. Murry's chemical messes than something to eat. In a dilapidated Boston rocker sat a plump little woman. She wasn't Mrs. Whatsit, so she must, Meg decided, be one of Mrs. Whatsit's two friends. She wore enormous spectacles, twice as thick and twice as large as Meg's and she was sewing busily, with rapid jabbing stitches, on a sheet. Several other sheets lay on the dusty floor.

Charles Wallace went up to her. "I really don't think you ought to have taken Mrs. Buncombe's sheets without consulting me," he said, as cross and bossy as only a very small boy can be. "What on earth do you want them for?"

The plump little woman beamed at him. "Why, Charlsie, my pet! *Le coeur a ses raisons que la raison ne connait point.* French. Pascal. *The heart has its reasons, whereof reason knows nothing.*"

"But that's not appropriate at all," Charles said crossly.

"Your mother would find it so." A smile seemed to gleam through the roundness of spectacles.

"I'm not talking about my mother's feelings about my father," Charles Wallace scolded. "I'm talking about Mrs. Buncombe's sheets."

The little woman sighed. The enormous glasses caught the light again and shone like an owl's eyes. "In case we need ghosts, of course," she said. "I should think you'd have guessed. If we have to frighten anybody away Whatsit thought we ought to do it appropriately. That's why it's so much fun to stay in a haunted house. But we really didn't mean you to know about the sheets. *Auf frischer Tat ertappt.* German. *In flagrante delicto.* Latin. *Caught in the act.* English. As I was saying—"

But Charles Wallace held up his hand in a peremptory gesture. "Mrs. Who, do you know this boy?"

Calvin bowed. "Good afternoon, Ma'am. I didn't quite catch your name."

"Mrs. Who will do," the woman said. "He wasn't my idea, Charlsie, but I think he's a good one."

"Where's Mrs. Whatsit?" Charles asked.

"She's busy. It's getting near time, Charlsie, getting near time. *Ab honesto virum bonum nihil deterret.* Seneca. *Nothing deters a good man from doing what is honorable.* And he's a very good man, Charlsie, darling, but right now he needs our help."

"Who?" Meg demanded.

"And little Megsie! Lovely to meet you, sweetheart. Your father, of course. Now go home, loves. The time is not yet ripe. Don't worry, we won't go without you. Get plenty of food and rest. Feed Calvin up. Now, off with you! *Justitiae soror fides.* Latin again, of course. *Faith is the sister of justice.* Trust in us! Now, shoo!" And she fluttered up from her chair and pushed them out the door with surprising power.

"Charles," Meg said. "I don't understand."

Charles took her by the hand and dragged her away from the house. Fortinbras ran on ahead, and Calvin was close behind them. "No," he said, "I don't either, yet. Not quite. I'll tell you what I know as soon as I can. But you saw Fort, didn't you? Not a growl. Not a quiver. Just as though there weren't anything strange about it. So you know it's okay. Look, do me a favor, both of you. Let's not talk about it till we've had something to eat. I need fuel so I can sort things out and assimilate them properly."

"Lead on, moron," Calvin cried gaily. "I've never even seen your house, and I have the funniest feeling that for the first time in my life I'm going home!"

Chapter 3

MRS. WHICH

In the forest evening was already beginning to fall, and they walked in silence. Charles and Fortinbras gamboled on ahead. Calvin walked with Meg, his fingers barely touching her arm in a protective gesture.

This has been the most impossible, the most confusing afternoon of my life, she thought, yet I don't feel confused or upset anymore; I only feel happy. Why?

"Maybe we weren't meant to meet before this," Calvin said. "I mean, I knew who you were in school and everything, but I didn't know you. But I'm glad we've met now, Meg. We're going to be friends, you know."

"I'm glad, too," Meg whispered, and they were silent again.

When they got back to the house Mrs. Murry was still in the lab. She was watching a pale blue fluid move slowly through a tube from a beaker to a retort. Over a Bunsen burner bubbled a big, earthenware dish of stew. "Don't tell Sandy and

Dennys I'm cooking out here," she said. "They're always suspicious that a few chemicals may get in with the meat, but I had an experiment I wanted to stay with."

"This is Calvin O'Keefe, Mother," Meg said. "Is there enough for him, too? It smells super."

"Hello, Calvin," Mrs. Murry shook hands with him. "Nice to meet you. We aren't having anything but stew tonight, but it's a good thick one."

"Sounds wonderful to me," Calvin said. "May I use your phone so my mother'll know where I am?"

"Of course. Show him where it is, will you, please, Meg? I won't ask you to use the one out here, if you don't mind. I'd like to finish up this experiment."

Meg led the way into the house. Charles Wallace and Fortinbras had gone off. Outdoors she could hear Sandy and Dennys hammering at the fort they were building up in one of the maples. "This way." Meg went through the kitchen and into the living room.

"I don't know why I call her when I don't come home," Calvin said, his voice bitter. "She wouldn't notice." He sighed and dialed. "Ma?" he said. "Oh, Hinky. Tell Ma I won't be home till late. Now don't forget. I don't want to be locked out again." He hung up, looked at Meg. "Do you know how lucky you are?"

She smiled rather wryly. "Not most of the time."

"A mother like that! A house like this! Gee, your mother's gorgeous! You should see my mother. She had all her upper teeth out and Pop got her a plate but she won't wear it, and most days she doesn't even comb her hair. Not that it makes much difference when she does." He clenched his fists. "But I love her. That's the funny part of it. I love them all, and they don't give a hoot about me. Maybe that's why I call when I'm not going to be home. Because I care. Nobody else does. You don't know how lucky you are to be loved."

Meg said in a startled way, "I guess I never thought of that. I guess I just took it for granted."

Calvin looked somber; then his enormous smile lit up his face again. "Things are going to happen, Meg! Good things! I feel it!" He began wandering, still slowly, around the pleasant, if shabby, living room. He stopped before a picture on the piano of a small group of men standing together on a beach. "Who's this?"

"Oh, a bunch of scientists."

"Where?"

Meg went over to the picture. "Cape Canaveral. This one's Father."

"Which?"

"Here."

"The one with glasses?"

"Yup. The one who needs a haircut." Meg giggled, forgetting her worries in her pleasure at showing Calvin the picture. "His hair's sort of the same color as mine, and he keeps forgetting to have it cut. Mother usually ends up doing it for him—she bought clippers and stuff—because he won't take the time to go to the barber."

Calvin studied the picture. "I like him," he announced judiciously. "Looks kind of like Charles Wallace, doesn't he?"

Meg laughed again. "When Charles was a baby he looked *exactly* like Father. It was really funny."

Calvin continued to look at the picture. "He's not handsome or anything. But I like him."

Meg was indignant. "He is too handsome."

Calvin shook his head. "Nah. He's tall and skinny like me."

"Well, I think you're handsome," Meg said. "Father's eyes are kind of like yours, too. You know. Really blue. Only you don't notice his as much because of the glasses."

"Where is he now?"

Meg stiffened. But she didn't have to answer because the door from lab to kitchen slammed, and Mrs. Murry came in, carrying a dish of stew. "Now," she called, "I'll finish this up properly on the stove. Have you done your homework, Meg?"

"Not quite," Meg said, going back into the kitchen.

"Then I'm sure Calvin won't mind if you finish before dinner."

"Sure, go ahead." Calvin fished in his pocket and pulled out a wad of folded paper. "As a matter of fact I have some junk of mine to finish up. Math. That's one thing I have a hard time keeping up in. I'm okay on anything to do with words, but I don't do as well with numbers."

Mrs. Murry smiled. "Why don't you get Meg to help you?"

"But, see, I'm several grades above Meg."

"Try asking her to help you with your math, anyhow," Mrs. Murry suggested.

"Well, sure," Calvin said. "Here. But it's pretty complicated."

Meg smoothed out the paper and studied it. "Do they care *how* you do it?" she asked. "I mean, can you work it out your own way?"

"Well, sure, as long as I understand and get the answers right."

"Well, *we* have to do it *their* way. Now look, Calvin, don't you see how much easier it would be if you did it *this* way?" Her pencil flew over the paper.

"Hey!" Calvin said. "Hey! I think I get it. Show

me once more on another one."

Again Meg's pencil was busy. "All you have to remember is that every ordinary fraction can be converted into an infinite periodic decimal fraction. See? So 3/7 is 0.428571."

"This is the craziest family." Calvin grinned at her. "I suppose I should stop being surprised by now, but you're supposed to be dumb in school, always being called up on the carpet."

"Oh, I am."

"The trouble with Meg and math," Mrs. Murry said briskly, "is that Meg and her father used to play with numbers and Meg learned far too many short cuts. So when they want her to do problems the long way around at school she gets sullen and stubborn and sets up a fine mental block for herself."

"Are there any more morons like Meg and Charles around?" Calvin asked. "If so, I should meet more of them."

"It might also help if Meg's handwriting were legible," Mrs. Murry said. "With a good deal of difficulty I can usually decipher it, but I doubt very much if her teachers can, or are willing to take the time. I'm planning on giving her a typewriter for Christmas. That may be a help."

"If I get anything right nobody'll believe it's me," Meg said.

"What's a megaparsec?" Calvin asked.

"One of Father's nicknames for me," Meg said. "It's also 3.26 million light years."

"What's $E = mc^2$?"

"Einstein's equation."

"What's E stand for?"

"Energy."

"m?"

"Mass."

"c^2?"

"The square of the velocity of light in centimeters per second."

"By what countries is Peru bounded?"

"I haven't the faintest idea. I think it's in South America somewhere."

"What's the capital of New York?"

"Well, New York City, of course!"

"Who wrote Boswell's *Life of Johnson?*"

"Oh, Calvin, I'm not any good at English."

Calvin groaned and turned to Mrs. Murry. "I see what you mean. Her I wouldn't want to teach."

"She's a little one-sided, I grant you," Mrs. Murry said, "though I blame her father and myself for that. She still enjoys playing with her dolls' house, though."

"*Mother!*" Meg shrieked in agony.

"Oh, darling, I'm sorry," Mrs. Murry said swiftly. "But I'm sure Calvin understands what I mean."

With a sudden enthusiastic gesture Calvin flung his arms out wide, as though he were embracing Meg and her mother, the whole house. "How did all this happen? Isn't it wonderful? I feel as though I were just being born! I'm not alone any more! Do you realize what that means to me?"

"But you're good at basketball and things," Meg protested. "You're good in school. Everybody likes you."

"For all the most unimportant reasons," Calvin said. "There hasn't been anybody, anybody in the world I could talk to. Sure, I can function on the same level as everybody else, I can hold myself down, but it isn't me."

Meg took a batch of forks from the drawer and turned them over and over, looking at them. "I'm all confused again."

"Oh, so 'm I," Calvin said gaily. "But now at least I know we're going somewhere."

Meg was pleased and a little surprised when the twins were excited at having Calvin for supper. They knew more about his athletic record and were far more impressed by it than she. Calvin ate five bowls of stew, three saucers of Jello™, and a dozen cookies, and then Charles Wallace insisted that Calvin take him up to bed and read to him. The twins, who had finished their homework, were allowed to watch half an hour of TV. Meg helped her mother with the dishes and then sat at the table and struggled with her homework. But she could not concentrate.

"Mother, are you upset?" she asked suddenly.

Mrs. Murry looked up from a copy of an English scientific magazine through which she was leafing. For a moment she did not speak. Then, "Yes."

"Why?"

Again Mrs. Murry paused. She held her hands out and looked at them. They were long and strong and beautiful. She touched with the fingers of her right hand the broad gold band on the third finger of her left hand. "I'm still quite a young woman, you know," she said finally, "though I realize that that's difficult for you children to conceive. And I'm still very much in love with your father. I miss him quite dreadfully."

"And you think all this has something to do with Father?"

"I think it must have."

"But what?"

"That I don't know. But it seems the only explanation."

"Do you think things always have an explanation?"

"Yes. I believe that they do. But I think that with our human limitations we're not always able to understand the explanations. But you see, Meg, just because we don't understand doesn't mean that the explanation doesn't exist."

"I like to understand things," Meg said.

"We all do. But it isn't always possible."

"Charles Wallace understands more than the rest of us, doesn't he?"

"Yes."

"Why?"

"I suppose because he's—well, because he's different, Meg."

"Different how?"

"I'm not quite sure. You know yourself he's not like anybody else."

"No. And I wouldn't want him to be," Meg said defensively.

"Wanting doesn't have anything to do with it. Charles Wallace is what he is. Different. New."

"New?"

"Yes. That's what your father and I feel."

Meg twisted her pencil so hard that it broke. She laughed. "I'm sorry. I'm really not being destructive. I'm just trying to get things straight."

"I know."

"But Charles Wallace doesn't *look* different from anybody else."

"No, Meg, but people are more than just the way they look. Charles Wallace's difference isn't physical. It's in essence."

Meg sighed heavily, took off her glasses and twirled them, put them back on again. "Well, I know Charles Wallace is different, and I know he's something *more*. I guess I'll just have to accept it without understanding it."

Mrs. Murry smiled at her. "Maybe that's really the point I was trying to put across."

"Yah," Meg said dubiously.

Her mother smiled again. "Maybe that's why our visitor last night didn't surprise me. Maybe that's why I'm able to have a—a willing suspension of disbelief. Because of Charles Wallace."

"Are *you* like Charles?" Meg asked.

"I? Heavens no. I'm blessed with more brains and opportunities than many people, but there's nothing about me that breaks out of the ordinary mold."

"Your looks do," Meg said.

Mrs. Murry laughed. "You just haven't had enough basis for comparison, Meg. I'm very ordinary, really."

Calvin O'Keefe, coming in then, said, "Ha ha."

"Charles all settled?" Mrs. Murry asked.

"Yes."

"What did you read to him?"

"Genesis. His choice. By the way, what kind of an experiment were you working on this afternoon, Mrs. Murry?"

"Oh, something my husband and I were cooking up together. I don't want to be *too* far behind him when he gets back."

"Mother," Meg pursued. "Charles says I'm not one thing or the other, not flesh nor fowl nor good red herring."

"Oh, for crying out loud," Calvin said, "you're *Meg*, aren't you? Come on and let's go for a walk."

But Meg was still not satisfied. "And what do you make of Calvin?" she demanded of her mother.

Mrs. Murry laughed. "I don't want to make anything of Calvin. I like him very much, and I'm delighted he's found his way here."

"Mother, you were going to tell me about a tesseract."

"Yes." A troubled look came into Mrs. Murry's eyes. "But not now, Meg. Not now. Go on out for that walk with Calvin. I'm going up to kiss Charles and then I have to see that the twins get to bed."

Outdoors the grass was wet with dew. The moon was halfway up and dimmed the stars for a great arc. Calvin reached out and took Meg's hand with a gesture as simple and friendly as Charles Wallace's. "Were you upsetting your mother?" he asked gently.

"I don't think *I* was. But she's upset."

"What about?"

"Father."

Calvin led Meg across the lawn. The shadows of the trees were long and twisted and there was a heavy, sweet, autumnal smell to the air. Meg stumbled as the land sloped suddenly downhill, but Calvin's strong hand steadied her. They walked carefully across the twins' vegetable garden, picking their way through rows of cabbages, beets, broccoli, pumpkins. Looming on their left were the tall stalks of corn. Ahead of them was a small apple orchard bounded by a stone wall, and beyond this the woods through which they had walked that afternoon. Calvin led the way to the wall, and then sat there, his red hair shining silver in the moonlight, his body dappled with patterns from the tangle of branches. He reached up, pulled an apple off a gnarled limb, and handed it to Meg, then picked one for himself. "Tell me about your father."

"He's a physicist."

"Sure, we all know that. And he's supposed to have left your mother and gone off with some dame."

Meg jerked up from the stone on which she was perched, but Calvin grabbed her by the wrist and pulled her back down. "Hold it, kid. I didn't say anything you hadn't heard already, did I?"

"No," Meg said, but continued to pull away. "Let me go."

"Come on, calm down. *You* know it isn't true, *I* know it isn't true. And how *any*body after one look at your mother could believe any man would leave her for another woman just shows how far jealousy will make people go. Right?"

"I guess so," Meg said, but her happiness had fled and she was back in a morass of anger and resentment.

"Look, dope." Calvin shook her gently. "I just want to get things straight, sort of sort out the fact from fiction. Your father's a physicist. That's a fact, yes?"

"Yes."

"He's a Ph.D. several times over."

"Yes."

"Most of the time he works alone but some of the time he was at the Institute for Higher Learning in Princeton. Correct?"

"Yes."

"Then he did some work for the government, didn't he?"

"Yes."

"You take it from there. That's all I know."

"That's about all I know, too," Meg said. "Maybe Mother knows more. I don't know. What he did was—well, it was what they call Classified."

"Top Secret, you mean?"

"That's right."

"And you don't even have any idea what it was about?"

Meg shook her head. "No. Not really. Just an idea because of where he was."

"Well, where?"

"Out in New Mexico for a while; we were with him there; and then he was in Florida at Cape Canaveral, and we were with him there, too. And then he was going to be traveling a lot, so we came here."

"You'd always had this house?"

"Yes. But we used to live in it just in the summer."

"And you don't know where your father was sent?"

"No. At first we got lots of letters. Mother and Father always wrote each other every day. I think Mother still writes him every night. Every once in a while the postmistress makes some kind of a crack about all her letters."

"I suppose they think she's pursuing him or something," Calvin said, rather bitterly. "They can't understand plain, ordinary love when they see it. Well, go on. What happened next?"

"Nothing happened," Meg said. "That's the trouble."

"Well, what about your father's letters?"

"They just stopped coming."

"You haven't heard anything at all?"

"No," Meg said. "Nothing." Her voice was heavy with misery.

Silence fell between them, as tangible as the dark tree shadows that fell across their laps and that now seemed to rest upon them as heavily as though they possessed a measurable weight of their own.

At last Calvin spoke in a dry, unemotional voice, not looking at Meg. "Do you think he could be dead?"

Again Meg leaped up, and again Calvin pulled her down. "No! They'd have told us if he were dead! There's always a telegram or something. They always tell you!"

"What *do* they tell you?"

Meg choked down a sob, managed to speak over it. "Oh, Calvin, Mother's tried and tried to find out. She's been down to Washington and everything. And all they'll say is that he's on a secret and dangerous mission, and she can be very proud of him, but he won't be able to—to communicate with us for a while. And they'll give us news as soon as they have it."

"Meg, don't get mad, but do you think maybe *they* don't know?"

A slow tear trickled down Meg's cheek. "That's what I'm afraid of."

"Why don't you cry?" Calvin asked gently. "You're just crazy about your father, aren't you? Go ahead and cry. It'll do you good."

Meg's voice came out trembling over tears. "I cry much too much. I should be like Mother. I should be able to control myself."

"Your mother's a completely different person and she's a lot older than you are."

"I wish I were a different person," Meg said shakily. "I hate myself."

Calvin reached over and took off her glasses. Then he pulled a handkerchief out of his pocket and wiped her tears. This gesture of tenderness undid her completely, and she put her head down on her knees and sobbed. Calvin sat quietly beside her, every once in a while patting her head. "I'm sorry," she sobbed finally. "I'm terribly sorry. Now you'll hate me."

"Oh, Meg, you *are* a moron," Calvin said. "Don't you know you're the nicest thing that's happened to me in a long time?"

Meg raised her head, and moonlight shone on her tearstained face; without the glasses her eyes were unexpectedly beautiful. "If Charles Wallace is a sport, I think I'm a biological mistake." Moonlight flashed against her braces as she spoke.

Now she was waiting to be contradicted. But Calvin said, "Do you know that this is the first time I've seen you without your glasses?"

"I'm blind as a bat without them. I'm near-sighted, like Father."

"Well, you know what, you've got dream-boat eyes," Calvin said. "Listen, you go right on wearing your glasses. I don't think I want anybody else to see what gorgeous eyes you have."

Meg smiled with pleasure. She could feel herself blushing and she wondered if the blush would be visible in the moonlight.

"Okay, hold it, you two," came a voice out of the shadows. Charles Wallace stepped into the moonlight. "I wasn't spying on you," he said quickly, "and I hate to break things up, but this is it, kids, this is it!" His voice quivered with excitement.

"This is what?" Calvin asked.

"We're going."

"Going? Where?" Meg reached out and instinctively grabbed for Calvin's hand.

"I don't know exactly," Charles Wallace said. "But I think it's to find Father."

Suddenly two eyes seemed to spring at them out of the darkness; it was the moonlight striking on Mrs. Who's glasses. She was standing next to Charles Wallace, and how she had managed to appear where a moment ago there had been nothing but flickering shadows in the moonlight Meg had no idea. She heard a sound behind her and turned around. There was Mrs. Whatsit scrambling over the wall.

"My, but I wish there were no wind," Mrs. Whatsit said plaintively. "It's so *difficult* with all these clothes." She wore her outfit of the night before, rubber boots and all, with the addition of one of Mrs. Buncombe's sheets which she had draped over her. As she slid off the wall the sheet caught in a low branch and came off. The felt hat slipped over both eyes, and another branch plucked at the pink stole. "Oh, *dear,*" she sighed. "I shall *never* learn to manage."

Mrs. Who wafted over to her, tiny feet scarcely seeming to touch the ground, the lenses of her glasses glittering. "*Come t'è picciol fallo amaro morso!* Dante. *What grievous pain a little fault doth give thee!*" With a clawlike hand she pushed the hat up on Mrs. Whatsit's forehead, untangled the stole from the tree, and with a deft gesture took the sheet and folded it.

"Oh, *thank* you," Mrs. Whatsit said. "You're *so* clever!"

"*Un asno viejo sabe más que un potro.* A. Perez. *An old ass knows more than a young colt.*"

"Just because you're a paltry few billion years—" Mrs. Whatsit was starting indignantly, when a sharp, strange voice cut in.

"Alll rrightt, girrllss. Thiss iss nno ttime forr bbickkerring."

"It's Mrs. Which," Charles Wallace said.

There was a faint gust of wind, the leaves shivered in it, the patterns of moonlight shifted, and in a circle of silver something shimmered, quivered, and the voice said, "I ddo nott thinkk I willl matterrialize commpletely. I ffindd itt verry ttirinngg, andd wee hhave mmuch ttoo ddoo."

Chapter 4

THE BLACK THING

The trees were lashed into a violent frenzy. Meg screamed and clutched at Calvin, and Mrs. Which's authoritative voice called out, "Qquiett, chilldd!"

Did a shadow fall across the moon or did the moon simply go out, extinguished as abruptly and completely as a candle? There was still the sound of leaves, a terrified, terrifying rushing. All light was gone. Darkness was complete. Suddenly the wind was gone, and all sound. Meg felt that Calvin was being torn from her. When she reached for him her fingers touched nothing.

She screamed out, "Charles!" and whether it was to help him or for him to help her, she did not know. The word was flung back down her throat and she choked on it.

She was completely alone.

She had lost the protection of Calvin's hand. Charles was nowhere, either to save or to turn to. She was alone in a fragment of nothingness. No light, no sound, no feeling. Where was her body? She tried to move in her panic, but there was nothing to move. Just as light and sound had vanished, she was gone, too. The corporeal Meg simply was not.

Then she felt her limbs again. Her legs and arms were tingling faintly, as though they had been asleep. She blinked her eyes rapidly, but though she herself was somehow back, nothing else was. It was not as simple as darkness, or absence of light. Darkness has a tangible quality; it can be moved through and felt; in darkness you can bark your shins; the world of things still exists around you. She was lost in a horrifying void.

It was the same way with the silence. This was more than silence. A deaf person can feel vibrations. Here there was nothing to feel.

Suddenly she was aware of her heart beating rapidly within the cage of her ribs. Had it stopped before? What had made it start again? The tingling in her arms and legs grew stronger, and suddenly she felt movement. This movement, she felt, must be the turning of the earth, rotating on its axis, traveling its elliptic course about the sun. And this feeling of moving with the earth was somewhat like the feeling of being in the ocean, out in the ocean beyond this rising and falling of the breakers, lying on the moving water, pulsing gently with the swells, and feeling the gentle, inexorable tug of the moon.

I am asleep; I am dreaming, she thought. I'm having a nightmare. I want to wake up. Let me wake up.

"Well!" Charles Wallace's voice said. "That was quite a trip! I do think you might have warned us."

Light began to pulse and quiver. Meg blinked and shoved shakily at her glasses and there was Charles Wallace standing indignantly in front of her, his hands on his hips. "Meg!" he shouted. "Calvin! Where are you?"

She saw Charles, she heard him, but she could not go to him. She could not shove through the strange, trembling light to meet him.

Calvin's voice came as though it were pushing through a cloud. "Well, just give me time, will you? I'm older than you are."

Meg gasped. It wasn't that Calvin wasn't there and then that he was. It wasn't that part of him came first and then the rest of him followed, like a hand and then an arm, an eye and then a nose. It was a sort of shimmering, a looking at Calvin through water, through smoke, through fire, and then there he was, solid and reassuring.

"Meg!" Charles Wallace's voice came. "Meg! Calvin, where's Meg?"

"I'm right here," she tried to say, but her voice seemed to be caught at its source.

"Meg!" Calvin cried, and he turned around, looking about wildly.

"Mrs. Which, you haven't left Meg be*hind*, have you?" Charles Wallace shouted.

"If you've hurt Meg, any of you—" Calvin started, but suddenly Meg felt a violent push and a shattering as though she had been thrust through a wall of glass.

"Oh, *there* you are!" Charles Wallace said, and rushed over to her and hugged her.

"But *where* am I?" Meg asked breathlessly, relieved to hear that her voice was now coming out of her in more or less a normal way.

She looked around rather wildly. They were standing in a sunlit field, and the air about them was moving with the delicious fragrance that comes only on the rarest of spring days when the sun's touch is gentle and the apple blossoms are just beginning to unfold. She pushed her glasses up on her nose to reassure herself that what she was seeing was real.

They had left the silver glint of a biting autumn evening; and now around them everything was golden with light. The grasses of the field were a tender new green, and scattered about were tiny, multicolored flowers. Meg turned slowly to face a mountain reaching so high into the sky that its peak was lost in a crown of puffy white clouds. From the trees at the base of the mountain came a sudden singing of birds. There was an air of such ineffable peace and joy all around her that her heart's wild thumping slowed.

> "When shall we three meet again,
> In thunder, lightning, or in rain,"

came Mrs. Who's voice. Suddenly the three of them were there, Mrs. Whatsit with her pink stole askew; Mrs. Who with her spectacles gleaming; and Mrs. Which still little more than a shimmer. Delicate, multicolored butterflies were fluttering about them, as though in greeting.

Mrs. Whatsit and Mrs. Who began to giggle, and they giggled until it seemed that, whatever their private joke was, they would fall down with the wild fun of it. The shimmer seemed to be laughing, too. It became vaguely darker and more solid; and then there appeared a figure in a black robe and a black peaked hat, beady eyes, a beaked nose, and long gray hair; one bony claw clutched a broomstick.

"Wwell, jusstt ttoo kkeepp yyou girrlls happpy," the strange voice said, and Mrs. Whatsit and Mrs. Who fell into each other's arms in gales of laughter.

"If you ladies have had your fun I think you should tell Calvin and Meg a little more about all this," Charles Wallace said coldly. "You scared Meg half out of her wits, whisking her off this way without any warning."

"*Finxerunt animi, raro et perpauca loquentis,*" Mrs. Who intoned. "Horace. *To action little, less to words inclined.*"

"Mrs. Who, I wish you'd stop quoting!" Charles Wallace sounded very annoyed.

Mrs. Whatsit adjusted her stole. "But she finds it so difficult to verbalize, Charles dear. It helps her if she can quote instead of working out words of her own."

"Anndd wee mussttn'tt looose ourr sensses of hummorr," Mrs. Which said. "Thee onnlly wway ttoo ccope withh ssometthingg ddeadly sseriouss iss ttoo ttry ttoo trreatt itt a llittlle lligghtly."

"But that's going to be hard for Meg," Mrs. Whatsit said. "It's going to be hard for her to realize that we *are* serious."

"What about me?" Calvin asked.

"The life of your father isn't at stake," Mrs. Whatsit told him.

"What about Charles Wallace, then?"

Mrs. Whatsit's unoiled-door-hinge voice was warm with affection and pride. "Charles Wallace knows. Charles Wallace knows that it's far more than just the life of his father. Charles Wallace knows what's at stake."

"But remember," Mrs. Who said, "*Αεηπου οὐδὲν, πὰντα δ' εηπίζειν χρεωτ.* Euripides. *Nothing is hopeless; we must hope for everything.*"

"Where are we now, and how did we get here?" Calvin asked.

"Uriel, the third planet of the star Malak in the spiral nebula Messier 101."

"This I'm supposed to believe?" Calvin asked indignantly.

"Aas yyou llike," Mrs. Which said coldly.

For some reason Meg felt that Mrs. Which, despite her looks and ephemeral broomstick, was someone in whom one could put complete trust. "It doesn't seem any more peculiar than anything else that's happened."

"Well, then, someone just tell me how we got here!" Calvin's voice was still angry and his freckles seemed to stand out on his face. "Even traveling at the speed of light it would take us years and years to get here."

"Oh, we don't travel at the speed of *anything*," Mrs. Whatsit explained earnestly. "We *tesser*. Or you might say, we *wrinkle*."

"Clear as mud," Calvin said.

Tesser, Meg thought. Could that have anything to do with Mother's tesseract?

She was about to ask when Mrs. Which started to speak, and one did not interrupt when Mrs. Which was speaking. "Mrs. Whatsit iss yyoungg andd nnaïve."

"She keeps thinking she can explain things in *words*," Mrs. Who said. *"Qui plus sait, plus se tait.* French, you know. *The more a man knows, the less he talks."*

"But she has to use words for Meg and Calvin," Charles reminded Mrs. Who. "If you brought them along, they have a right to know what's going on."

Meg went up to Mrs. Which. In the intensity of her question she had forgotten all about the tesseract. "Is my father here?"

Mrs. Which shook her head. "Nnott heeere, Megg. Llett Mrs. Whatsitt expllainn. Shee isss yyoungg annd thee llanguage of worrds iss eeasierr fforr hherr thann itt iss fforr Mrs. Whoo andd mee."

"We stopped here," Mrs. Whatsit explained,

"more or less to catch our breaths. And to give you a chance to know what you're up against."

"But what about Father?" Meg asked. "Is he all right?"

"For the moment, love, yes. He's one of the reasons we're here. But you see, he's only one."

"Well, where is he? Please take me to him!"

"We can't, not yet," Charles said. "You have to be patient, Meg."

"But I'm *not* patient!" Meg cried passionately. "I've never been patient!"

Mrs. Who's glasses shone at her gently. "If you want to help your father then you must learn patience. *Vitam impendere vero. To stake one's life for the truth.* That is what we must do."

"That is what your father is doing." Mrs. Whatsit nodded, her voice, like Mrs. Who's, very serious, very solemn. Then she smiled her radiant smile. "Now! Why don't you three children wander around and Charles can explain things a little. You're perfectly safe on Uriel. That's why we stopped here to rest."

"But aren't you coming with us?" Meg asked fearfully.

There was silence for a moment. Then Mrs. Which raised her authoritative hand. "Sshoww themm," she said to Mrs. Whatsit, and at something in her voice Meg felt prickles of apprehension.

"*Now?*" Mrs. Whatsit asked, her creaky voice rising to a squeak. Whatever it was Mrs. Which wanted them to see, it was something that made Mrs. Whatsit uncomfortable, too.

"Nnoww," Mrs. Which said. "Tthey mmay aas welll knoww."

"Should—should I *change?*" Mrs. Whatsit asked.

"Bbetter."

"I hope it won't upset the children too much," Mrs. Whatsit murmured, as though to herself.

"Should I change, too?" Mrs. Who asked. "Oh, but I've had *fun* in these clothes. But I'll have to admit Mrs. Whatsit is the best at it. *Das Werk lobt den Meister.* German. *The work proves the craftsman.* Shall I transform now, too?"

Mrs. Which shook her head. "Nnott yett. Nnott heere. Yyou mmay wwaitt."

"Now, don't be frightened, loves," Mrs. Whatsit said. Her plump little body began to shimmer, to quiver, to shift. The wild colors of her clothes became muted, whitened. The pudding-bag shape stretched, lengthened, merged. And suddenly before the children was a creature more beautiful than any Meg had even imagined, and the beauty lay in far more than the outward description. Outwardly Mrs. Whatsit was surely no longer a Mrs. Whatsit. She was a marble white body with powerful flanks, something like a horse but at the same time completely unlike a horse, for from the magnificently modeled back sprang a nobly formed torso, arms, and a head resembling a man's, but a man with a perfection of dignity and virtue, an exaltation of joy such as Meg had never before seen. No, she thought, it's not like a Greek centaur. Not in the least.

From the shoulders slowly a pair of wings unfolded, wings made of rainbows, of light upon water, of poetry.

Calvin fell to his knees.

"No," Mrs. Whatsit said, though her voice was not Mrs. Whatsit's voice. "Not to me, Calvin. Never to me. Stand up."

"Ccarrry themm," Mrs. Which commanded.

With a gesture both delicate and strong Mrs. Whatsit knelt in front of the children, stretching her wings wide and holding them steady, but quivering. "Onto my back, now," the new voice said.

The children took hesitant steps toward the beautiful creature.

"But what do we call you now?" Calvin asked.

"Oh, my dears," came the new voice, a rich voice with the warmth of a woodwind, the clarity of a trumpet, the mystery of an English horn. "You can't go on changing my name each time I metamorphose. And I've had such pleasure being Mrs. Whatsit I think you'd better keep to that." She? he? it? smiled at them, and the radiance of the smile was as tangible as a soft breeze, as directly warming as the rays of the sun.

"Come." Charles Wallace clambered up.

Meg and Calvin followed him, Meg sitting between the two boys. A tremor went through the great wings and then Mrs. Whatsit lifted and they were moving through the air.

Meg soon found that there was no need to cling to Charles Wallace or Calvin. The great creature's flight was serenely smooth. The boys were eagerly looking around the landscape.

"Look." Charles Wallace pointed. "The mountains are so tall that you can't see where they end."

Meg looked upwards and indeed the mountains seemed to be reaching into infinity.

They left the fertile fields and flew across a great plateau of granite-like rock shaped into enormous monoliths. These had a definite, rhythmic form, but they were not statues; they were like nothing Meg had ever seen before, and she wondered if they had been made by wind and weather, by the formation of this earth, or if they were a creation of beings like the one on which she rode.

They left the great granite plain and flew over a

garden even more beautiful than anything in a dream. In it were gathered many of the creatures like the one Mrs. Whatsit had become, some lying among the flowers, some swimming in a broad, crystal river that flowed through the garden, some flying in what Meg was sure must be a kind of dance, moving in and out above the trees. They were making music, music that came not only from their throats but from the movement of their great wings as well.

"What are they singing?" Meg asked excitedly.

Mrs. Whatsit shook her beautiful head. "It won't go into your words. I can't possibly transfer it to your words. Are you getting any of it, Charles?"

Charles Wallace sat very still on the broad back, on his face an intently listening look, the look he had when he delved into Meg or his mother. "A little. Just a very little. But I think I could get more in time."

"Yes. You could learn it, Charles. But there isn't time. We can only stay here long enough to rest up and make a few preparations."

Meg hardly listened to her. "I want to know what they're saying! I want to know what it means."

"Try, Charles," Mrs. Whatsit urged. "Try to translate. You can let yourself go, now. You don't have to hold back."

"But I can't!" Charles Wallace cried in an anguished voice. "I don't know enough! Not yet!"

"Then try to work with me and I'll see if I can't verbalize it a little for them."

Charles Wallace got his look of probing, of listening.

I know that look! Meg thought suddenly. Now I think I know what it means! Because I've had it myself, sometimes, doing math with Father, when a problem is just about to come clear—

Mrs. Whatsit seemed to be listening to Charles's thoughts. "Well, yes, that's an idea. I can try. Too bad you don't really know it so you can give it to me direct, Charles. It's so much more work this way."

"Don't be lazy," Charles said.

Mrs. Whatsit did not take offense. She explained, "Oh, it's my favorite kind of work, Charles. That's why they chose me to go along, even though I'm so much younger. It's my one real talent. But it takes a tremendous amount of energy, and we're going to need every ounce of energy for what's ahead of us. But I'll try. For Calvin and Meg I'll try." She was silent; the great wings almost stopped moving; only a delicate stirring seemed to keep them aloft. "Listen, then," Mrs. Whatsit said. The resonant voice rose and the words seemed to be all around them so that Meg felt that she could almost reach out and touch them: *"Sing unto the Lord a new song, and his praise from the end of the earth, ye that go down to the sea, and all that is therein; the isles, and the inhabitants thereof. Let the wilderness and the cities thereof lift their voice; let the inhabitants of the rock sing, let them shout from the top of the mountains. Let them give glory unto the Lord!"*

Throughout her entire body Meg felt a pulse of joy such as she had never known before. Calvin's hand reached out; he did not clasp her hand in his; he moved his fingers so that they were barely touching hers, but joy flowed through them, back and forth between them, around them and about them and inside them.

When Mrs. Whatsit sighed it seemed completely incomprehensible that through this bliss could come the faintest whisper of doubt.

"We must go now, children." Mrs. Whatsit's voice was deep with sadness, and Meg could not understand. Raising her head, Mrs. Whatsit gave a call that seemed to be a command, and one of the creatures flying above the trees nearest them raised its head to listen, and then flew off and picked three flowers from a tree growing near the river and brought them over. "Each of you take one," Mrs. Whatsit said. "I'll tell you how to use them later."

As Meg took her flower she realized that it was not a single blossom, but hundreds of tiny flowerets forming a kind of hollow bell.

"Where are we going?" Calvin asked.

"Up."

The wings moved steadily, swiftly. The garden was left behind, the stretch of granite, the mighty shapes, and then Mrs. Whatsit was flying upward, climbing steadily up, up. Below them the trees of the mountain dwindled, became sparse, were replaced by bushes and then small, dry grasses, and then vegetation ceased entirely and there were only rocks, points and peaks of rock, sharp and dangerous. "Hold on tight," Mrs. Whatsit said. "Don't slip."

Meg felt Calvin's arm circle her waist in a secure hold.

Still they moved upward.

Now they were in clouds. They could see nothing but drifting whiteness, and the moisture clung to them and condensed in icy droplets. As Meg shivered, Calvin's grip tightened. In front of her Charles Wallace sat quietly. Once he turned just long enough to give her a swift glance of tenderness and concern. But Meg felt as each moment passed that he was growing farther and farther away, that he was becoming less and less her adored baby brother and more and more one with whatever kind of being Mrs. Whatsit, Mrs. Who, and Mrs. Which in actuality were.

Abruptly they burst out of the clouds into a shaft of light. Below them there were still rocks; above them the rocks continued to reach up into the sky, but now, though it seemed miles upward, Meg could see where the mountain at last came to an end.

Mrs. Whatsit continued to climb, her wings straining a little. Meg felt her heart racing; cold sweat began to gather on her face and her lips felt as though they were turning blue. She began to gasp.

"All right, children, use your flowers now," Mrs. Whatsit said. "The atmosphere will continue to get thinner from now on. Hold the flowers up to your face and breathe through them and they will give you enough oxygen. It won't be as much as you're used to, but it will be enough."

Meg had almost forgotten the flowers, and was grateful to realize that she was still clasping them, that she hadn't let them fall from her fingers. She pressed her face into the blossoms and breathed deeply.

Calvin still held her with one arm, but he, too, held the flowers to his face.

Charles Wallace moved the hand with the flowers slowly, almost as though he were in a dream.

Mrs. Whatsit's wings strained against the thinness of the atmosphere. The summit was only a little way above them, and then they were there. Mrs. Whatsit came to rest on a small plateau of smooth silvery rock. There ahead of them was a great white disk.

"One of Uriel's moons," Mrs. Whatsit told them, her mighty voice faintly breathless.

"Oh, it's beautiful!" Meg cried. "It's beautiful!"

The silver light from the enormous moon poured over them, blending with the golden quality of the day, flowing over the children, over Mrs. Whatsit, over the mountain peak.

"Now we will turn around," Mrs. Whatsit said, and at the quality of her voice, Meg was afraid again.

But when they turned she saw nothing. Ahead of them was the thin clear blue of sky; below them the rocks thrusting out of the shifting sea of white clouds.

"Now we will wait," Mrs. Whatsit said, "for sunset and moonset."

Almost as she spoke the light began to deepen, to darken.

"I want to watch the moon set," Charles Wallace said.

"No, child. Do not turn around, any of you. Face out towards the dark. What I have to show you will be more visible then. Look ahead, straight ahead, as far as you can possibly look."

Meg's eyes ached from the strain of looking and seeing nothing. Then, above the clouds which encircled the mountain, she seemed to see a shadow, a faint thing of darkness so far off that she was scarcely sure she was really seeing it.

Charles Wallace said, "What's that?"

"That sort of shadow out there," Calvin gestured. "What is it? I don't like it."

"Watch," Mrs. Whatsit commanded.

It was a shadow, nothing but a shadow. It was not even as tangible as a cloud. Was it cast by something? Or was it a Thing in itself?

The sky darkened. The gold left the light and they were surrounded by blue, blue deepening until where there had been nothing but the evening sky there was now a faint pulse of star, and then another and another and another. There were more stars than Meg had ever seen before.

"The atmosphere is so thin here," Mrs. Whatsit said as though in answer to her unasked question, "that it does not obscure your vision as it would at home. Now look. Look straight ahead."

Meg looked. The dark shadow was still there. It had not lessened or dispersed with the coming of night. And where the shadow was the stars were not visible.

What could there be about a shadow that was so terrible that she knew that there had never been before or ever would be again, anything that would chill her with a fear that was beyond shuddering, beyond crying or screaming, beyond the possibility of comfort?

Meg's hand holding the blossoms slowly dropped and it seemed as though a knife gashed through her lungs. She gasped, but there was no air for her to breathe. Darkness glazed her eyes and mind, but as she started to fall into unconsciousness her head dropped down into the flowers which she was still clutching; and as she inhaled the fragrance of their purity her mind and body revived, and she sat up again.

The shadow was still there, dark and dreadful.

Calvin held her hand strongly in his, but she felt neither strength nor reassurance in his touch. Beside her a tremor went through Charles Wallace, but he sat very still.

He shouldn't be seeing this, Meg thought. This is too much for so little a boy, no matter how different and extraordinary a little boy.

Calvin turned, rejecting the dark Thing that blotted out the light of the stars. "Make it go away, Mrs. Whatsit," he whispered. "Make it go away. It's evil."

Slowly the great creature turned around so that the shadow was behind them, so that they saw only the stars unobscured, the soft throb of starlight on the mountain, the descending circle of the great moon swiftly slipping over the horizon. Then, without a word from Mrs. Whatsit, they were traveling downward, down, down. When they reached the corona of clouds Mrs. Whatsit said, "You can breathe without the flowers now, my children."

Silence again. Not a word. It was as though the shadow had somehow reached out with its dark power and touched them so that they were incapable of speech. When they got back to the flowery field, bathed now in starlight, and moonlight from another, smaller, yellower, rising moon, a little of the tenseness went out of their bodies, and they realized that the body of the beautiful creature on which they rode had been as rigid as theirs.

With a graceful gesture it dropped to the ground and folded its great wings. Charles Wallace was the first to slide off. "Mrs. Who! Mrs. Which!" he called, and there was an immediate quivering in the air. Mrs. Who's familiar glasses gleamed at them. Mrs. Which appeared, too; but, as she had told the children, it was difficult for her to materialize completely, and though there was the robe and peaked hat, Meg could look through them to mountain and stars. She slid off Mrs. Whatsit's back and walked, rather unsteadily after the long ride, over to Mrs. Which.

"That dark Thing we saw," she said. "Is that what my father is fighting?"

Chapter 5

THE TESSERACT

"Yes," Mrs. Which said. "Hhee iss beehindd thee ddarrkness, sso thatt eevenn wee cannott seee hhimm."

Meg began to cry, to sob aloud. Through her tears she could see Charles Wallace standing there, very small, very white. Calvin put his arms around her, but she shuddered and broke away, sobbing wildly. Then she was enfolded in the great wings of Mrs. Whatsit and she felt comfort and strength pouring through her. Mrs. Whatsit was not speaking aloud, and yet through the wings Meg understood words.

"My child, do not despair. Do you think we would have brought you here if there were no hope? We are asking you to do a difficult thing, but we are confident that you can do it. Your father needs help, he needs courage, and for his children he may be able to do what he cannot do for himself."

"Nnow," Mrs. Which said. "Arre wee rreaddy?"

"Where are we going?" Calvin asked.

Again Meg felt an actual physical tingling of fear as Mrs. Which spoke.

"Wwee musstt ggo bbehindd thee sshaddow."

"But we will not do it all at once," Mrs. Whatsit comforted them. "We will do it in short stages." She looked at Meg. "Now we will tesser, we will wrinkle again. Do you understand?"

"No," Meg said flatly.

Mrs. Whatsit sighed. "Explanations are not easy when they are about things for which your civilization still has no words. Calvin talked about traveling at the speed of light. You understand that, little Meg?"

"Yes," Meg nodded.

"That, of course, is the impractical, long way around. We have learned to take short cuts wherever possible."

"Sort of like in math?" Meg asked.

"Like in math." Mrs. Whatsit looked over at Mrs. Who. "Take your skirt and show them."

"*La experiencia es la madre de la ciencia.* Spanish, my dears. Cervantes. *Experience is the mother of knowledge.*" Mrs. Who took a portion of her white robe in her hands and held it tight.

"You see," Mrs. Whatsit said, "if a very small insect were to move from the section of skirt in Mrs. Who's right hand to that in her left, it would be quite a long walk for him if he had to walk straight across."

Swiftly Mrs. Who brought her hands, still holding the skirt, together.

"Now, you see," Mrs. Whatsit said, "he would *be* there, without that long trip. That is how we travel."

Charles Wallace accepted the explanation serenely. Even Calvin did not seem perturbed. "Oh, *dear*," Meg sighed. "I guess I *am* a moron. I just don't get it."

"That is because you think of space only in three dimensions," Mrs. Whatsit told her. "We travel in the fifth dimension. This is something you can understand, Meg. Don't be afraid to try. Was your mother able to explain a tesseract to you?"

"Well, she never did," Meg said. "She got so upset about it. Why, Mrs. Whatsit? She said it had something to do with her and Father."

"It was a concept they were playing with," Mrs. Whatsit said, "going beyond the fourth dimension to the fifth. Did your mother explain it to you, Charles?"

"Well, yes." Charles looked a little embarrassed. "Please don't be hurt, Meg. I just kept at her while you were at school till I got it out of her."

Meg sighed. "Just explain it to me."

"Okay," Charles said. "What is the first dimension?"

"Well—a line:———"

"Okay. And the second dimension?"

"Well, you'd square the line. A flat square would be in the second dimension."

"And the third?"

"Well, you'd square the second dimension. Then the square wouldn't be flat any more. It would have a bottom, and sides, and a top."

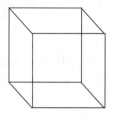

"And the fourth?"

"Well, I guess if you want to put it into mathematical terms you'd square the square. But you can't take a pencil and draw it the way you can the first three. I know it's got something to do with Einstein and time. I guess maybe you could call the fourth dimension Time."

"That's right," Charles said. "Good girl. Okay, then, for the fifth dimension you'd square the fourth, wouldn't you?"

"I guess so."

"Well, the fifth dimension's a tesseract. You add that to the other four dimensions and you can travel through space without having to go the long way around. In other words, to put it into Euclid, or old-fashioned plane geometry, a straight line is *not* the shortest distance between two points."

For a brief, illuminating second Meg's face had the listening, probing expression that was so often seen on Charles's. "I see!" she cried. "I got it! For just a moment I got it! I can't possibly explain it now, but there for a second I saw it!" She turned excitedly to Calvin. "Did you get it?"

He nodded. "Enough. I don't understand it the way Charles Wallace does, but enough to get the idea."

"Sso nnow wee ggo," Mrs. Which said. "Tthere iss nott all thee ttime inn tthe worrlld."

"Could we hold hands?" Meg asked.

Calvin took her hand and held it tightly in his.

"You can try," Mrs. Whatsit said, "though I'm not sure how it will work. You see, though we travel together, we travel alone. We will go first and take you afterward in the backwash. That may be easier for you." As she spoke the great white body began to waver, the wings to dissolve into mist. Mrs. Who seemed to evaporate until there was nothing but the glasses, and then the glasses, too, disappeared. It reminded Meg of the Cheshire Cat.

—I've often seen a face without glasses, she thought;—but glasses without a face! I wonder if I go that way, too. First me and then my glasses?

She looked over at Mrs. Which. Mrs. Which was there and then she wasn't.

There was a gust of wind and a great thrust and a sharp shattering as she was shoved through—what? Then darkness; silence; nothingness. If Calvin was still holding her hand she could not feel it. But this time she was prepared for the sudden and complete dissolution of her body. When she felt the tingling coming back to her fingertips she knew that this journey was almost over and she could feel again the pressure of Calvin's hand about hers.

Without warning, coming as a complete and unexpected shock, she felt a pressure she had never imagined, as though she were being completely flattened out by an enormous steam roller. This was far worse than the nothingness had been; while she was nothing there was no need to breathe, but now her lungs were squeezed together so that although she was dying for want of air there was no way for her lungs to expand and contract, to take in the air that she must have to stay alive. This was completely different from the thinning of atmosphere when they flew up the mountain and she had had to put the flowers to her face to breathe. She tried to gasp, but a paper doll can't gasp. She thought she was trying to think, but her flattened-out mind was as unable to function as her lungs; her thoughts were squashed along with the rest of her. Her heart tried to beat; it gave a knifelike, sidewise movement, but it could not expand.

But then she seemed to hear a voice, or if not a voice, at least words, words flattened out like printed words on paper, "Oh, no! We can't stop here! This is a *two*-dimensional planet and the children can't manage here!"

She was whizzed into nothingness again, and nothingness was wonderful. She did not mind that she could not feel Calvin's hand, that she could not see or feel or be. The relief from the intolerable pressure was all she needed.

Then the tingling began to come back to her fingers, her toes; she could feel Calvin holding her tightly. Her heart beat regularly; blood coursed through her veins. Whatever had happened, whatever mistake had been made, it was over now. She thought she heard Charles Wallace saying, his words round and full as spoken words ought to be, "*Really*, Mrs. Which, you might have killed us!"

This time she was pushed out of the frightening fifth dimension with a sudden, immediate jerk. There she was, herself again, standing with Calvin beside her, holding onto her hand for dear life, and Charles Wallace in front of her, looking indignant. Mrs. Whatsit, Mrs. Who, and Mrs. Which were not visible, but she knew that they were there; the fact of their presence was strong about her.

"Cchilldrenn, I appolloggize," came Mrs. Which's voice.

"Now, Charles, calm down," Mrs. Whatsit said, appearing not as the great and beautiful beast she had been when they last saw her, but in her familiar wild garb of shawls and scarves and the old tramp's coat and hat. "You know how difficult it is for her to materialize. If you are not substantial yourself it's *very* difficult to realize how limiting protoplasm is."

"I *ammm* ssorry," Mrs. Which's voice came again; but there was more than a hint of amusement in it.

"It is *not* funny." Charles Wallace gave a childish stamp of his foot.

Mrs. Who's glasses shone out, and the rest of her appeared more slowly behind them. "*We are such stuff as dreams are made on.*" She smiled broadly. "Prospero in *The Tempest*. I do like that play."

"You didn't do it on *purpose?*" Charles demanded.

"Oh, my darling, of course not," Mrs. Whatsit said quickly. "It was just a very understandable mistake. It's very difficult for Mrs. Which to think in a corporeal way. She wouldn't hurt you deliberately; you know that. And it's really a very pleasant little planet, and rather amusing to be flat. We always enjoy our visits there."

"Where are we now, then?" Charles Wallace demanded. "And why?"

"In Orion's belt. We have a friend here, and we want you to have a look at your own planet."

"When are we going home?" Meg asked anxiously. "What about Mother? What about the twins? They'll be terribly worried about us. When we didn't come in at bedtime—well, Mother must be frantic by now. She and the twins and Fort will have been looking and looking for us, and of course we aren't there to be found!"

"Now, don't worry, my pet," Mrs. Whatsit said cheerfully. "We took care of that before we left. Your mother has had enough to worry her with you and Charles to cope with, and not knowing about your father, without our adding to her anxieties. We took a time wrinkle as well as a space wrinkle. It's very easy to do if you just know how."

"What do you mean?" Meg asked plaintively. "Please, Mrs. Whatsit, it's all so confusing."

"Just relax and don't worry over things that needn't trouble you," Mrs. Whatsit said. "We made a nice, tidy little time tesser, and unless something goes terribly wrong we'll have you back about five minutes before you left, so there'll be time to spare and nobody'll ever need to know you were gone at all, though of course you'll be telling your mother, dear lamb that she is. And if something goes terribly wrong it won't matter whether we ever get back at all."

"Ddon'tt ffrrightenn themm," Mrs. Which's voice came. "Aare yyou llosingg ffaith?"

"Oh, no. No, I'm not."

But Meg thought her voice sounded a little faint.

"I hope *this* is a nice planet," Calvin said. "We can't *see* much of it. Does it ever clear up?"

Meg looked around her, realizing that she had been so breathless from the journey and the stop on the two-dimensional planet that she had not noticed her surroundings. And perhaps this was not very surprising, for the main thing about the surroundings was exactly that they *were* unnoticeable. They seemed to be standing on some kind of nondescript, flat surface. The air around them was gray. It was not exactly fog, but she could see nothing through it.

Visibility was limited to the nicely definite bodies of Charles Wallace and Calvin, the rather unbelievable bodies of Mrs. Whatsit and Mrs. Who, and a faint occasional glimmer that was Mrs. Which.

"Come, children," Mrs. Whatsit said. "We don't have far to go, and we might as well walk. It will do you good to stretch your legs a little."

As they moved through the grayness Meg caught an occasional glimpse of slaglike rocks, but there were no traces of trees or bushes, nothing but flat ground under their feet, no sign of any vegetation at all.

Finally, ahead of them there loomed what seemed to be a hill of stone. As they approached it Meg could see that there was an entrance that led into a deep, dark cavern. "Are we going in there?" she asked nervously.

"Don't be afraid," Mrs. Whatsit said. "It's easier for the Happy Medium to work within. Oh, you'll like her, children. She's very jolly. If ever I saw her looking unhappy I would be very depressed myself. As long as she can laugh I'm sure everything is going to come out right in the end."

"Mmrs. Whattsitt," came Mrs. Which's voice severely, "jusstt beccause yyou arre verry younngg iss nno exxcuse forr tallkingg tooo muchh."

Mrs. Whatsit looked hurt, but she subsided.

"Just how old *are* you?" Calvin asked her.

"Just a moment," Mrs. Whatsit murmured, and appeared to calculate rapidly upon her fingers. She nodded triumphantly. "Exactly 2,379,152,497 years, 8 months, and 3 days. That is according to *your* calendar, of course, which even you know isn't very accurate." She leaned closer to Meg and Calvin and whispered, "It was really a *very* great honor for me to be chosen for this mission. It's just because of my verbalizing and materializing so well, you know. But of course we can't take any credit for our talents. It's how we use them that counts. And I make far too many mistakes. That's why Mrs. Who and I enjoyed seeing Mrs. Which make a mistake when she tried to land you on a two-dimensional planet. It was *that* we were laughing at, not at you. She was laughing at herself, you see. She's really terribly nice to us younger ones."

Meg was listening with such interest to what Mrs. Whatsit was saying that she hardly noticed when they went into the cave; the transition from the grayness of outside to the grayness of inside was almost unnoticeable. She saw a flickering light ahead of them, ahead and down, and it was toward this that they went. As they drew closer she realized that it was a fire.

"It gets very cold in here," Mrs. Whatsit said, "so we asked her to have a good bonfire going for you."

As they approached the fire they could see a dark shadow against it, and as they went closer still they could see that the shadow was a woman. She wore a turban of beautiful pale mauve silk, and a long, flowing, purple satin gown. In her hands was a crystal ball into which she was gazing raptly. She did not appear to see the children, Mrs. Whatsit, Mrs. Who, and Mrs. Which, but continued to stare into the crystal ball; and as she stared she began to laugh; and she laughed and laughed at whatever it was that she was seeing.

Mrs. Which's voice rang out clear and strong, echoing against the walls of the cavern, and the words fell with a sonorous clang.

"Wwee arre Hherre!"

The woman looked up from the ball, and when she saw them she got up and curtsied deeply. Mrs.

Whatsit and Mrs. Who dropped small curtsies in return, and the shimmer seemed to bow slightly.

"Oh, Medium, dear," Mrs. Whatsit said, "these are the children. Charles Wallace Murry." Charles Wallace bowed. "Margaret Murry." Meg felt that if Mrs. Whatsit and Mrs. Who had curtsied, she ought to, also; so she did, rather awkwardly. "And Calvin O'Keefe." Calvin bobbed his head. "We want them to see their home planet," Mrs. Whatsit said.

The Medium lost the delighted smile she had worn till then. "Oh, *why* must you make me look at unpleasant things when there are so many delightful ones to see?"

Again Mrs. Which's voice reverberated through the cave. "Therre willl nno llonggerr bee sso manyy pplleasanntt thinggss too llookk att iff rressponssible ppeoplle ddo nnott ddo ssomethingg abboutt thee unnppleassanntt oness."

The Medium sighed and held the ball high.

"Look, children," Mrs. Whatsit said. "Look into it well."

"*Que la terre est petite à qui la voit des cieux!* Delille. *How small is the earth to him who looks from heaven,*" Mrs. Who intoned musically.

Meg looked into the crystal ball, at first with caution, then with increasing eagerness, as she seemed to see an enormous sweep of dark and empty space, and then galaxies swinging across it. Finally they seemed to move in closer on one of the galaxies.

"Your own Milky Way," Mrs. Whatsit whispered to Meg.

They were headed directly toward the center of the galaxy; then they moved off to one side; stars seemed to be rushing at them. Meg flung her arm up over her face as though to ward off the blow.

"Llookk!" Mrs. Which commanded.

Meg dropped her arm. They seemed to be moving in toward a planet. She thought she could make out polar ice caps. Everything seemed sparkling clear.

"No, no, Medium dear, that's Mars," Mrs. Whatsit reproved gently.

"Do I *have* to?" the Medium asked.

"NNOWW!" Mrs. Which commanded.

The bright planet moved out of their vision. For a moment there was the darkness of space; then another planet. The outlines of this planet were not clean and clear. It seemed to be covered with a smoky haze. Through the haze Meg thought she could make out the familiar outlines of continents like pictures in her Social Studies books.

"Is it because of our atmosphere that we can't see properly?" she asked anxiously.

"Nno, Mmegg, yyou knnoww thatt itt iss nnott tthee attmossspheeere," Mrs. Which said. "Yyou mmusstt bee brrave."

"It's the Thing!" Charles Wallace cried. "It's the Dark Thing we saw from the mountain peak on Uriel when we were riding on Mrs. Whatsit's back!"

"Did it just come?" Meg asked in agony, unable to take her eyes from the sickness of the shadow which darkened the beauty of the earth. "Did it just come while we've been gone?"

Mrs. Which's voice seemed very tired. "Ttell herr," she said to Mrs. Whatsit.

Mrs. Whatsit sighed. "No, Meg. It hasn't just come. It has been there for a great many years. That is why your planet is such a troubled one."

"But why—" Calvin started to ask, his voice croaking hoarsely.

Mrs. Whatsit raised her hand to silence him. "We showed you the Dark Thing on Uriel first—oh, for many reasons. First, because the atmosphere on the mountain peaks there is so clear and thin you could see it for what it is. And we thought it would be easier for you to understand it if you saw it—well, someplace *else* first, not your own earth."

"I hate it!" Charles Wallace cried passionately. "I hate the Dark Thing!"

Mrs. Whatsit nodded. "Yes, Charles dear. We all do. That's another reason we wanted to prepare you on Uriel. We thought it would be too frightening for you to see it first of all about your own, beloved world."

"But what is it?" Calvin demanded. "We know that it's evil, but what is it?"

"Yyouu hhave ssaidd itt!" Mrs. Which's voice rang out. "Itt iss Eevill. Itt iss thee Ppowers of Ddarrkknesss!"

"But what's going to happen?" Meg's voice trembled. "Oh, please, Mrs. Which, tell us what's going to happen!"

"Wee wwill cconnttinnue tto ffightt!"

Something in Mrs. Which's voice made all three of the children stand straighter, throwing back their shoulders with determination, looking at the glimmer that was Mrs. Which with pride and confidence.

"And we're not alone, you know, children," came Mrs. Whatsit, the comforter. "All through the universe it's being fought, all through the cosmos, and my, but it's a grand and exciting battle. I know it's hard for you to understand about size, how there's very little difference in the size of the tiniest microbe and the greatest galaxy. You think about that, and maybe it won't seem strange to you that some of our very best fighters have come right from your own planet, and it's a *little* planet, dears, out on the edge of a little galaxy. You can be proud that it's done so well."

"Who have our fighters been?" Calvin asked.

"Oh, *you* must know them, dear," Mrs. Whatsit said.

Mrs. Who's spectacles shone out at them triumphantly, *"And the light shineth in darkness; and the darkness comprehended it not."*

"Jesus!" Charles Wallace said. "Why of course, Jesus!"

"Of course!" Mrs. Whatsit said. "Go on, Charles, love. There were others. All your great artists. They've been lights for us to see by."

"Leonardo da Vinci?" Calvin suggested tentatively. "And Michelangelo?"

"And Shakespeare," Charles Wallace called out, "and Bach! And Pasteur and Madame Curie and Einstein!"

Now Calvin's voice rang with confidence. "And Schweitzer and Gandhi and Buddha and Beethoven and Rembrandt and St. Francis!"

"Now you, Meg," Mrs. Whatsit ordered.

"Oh, Euclid, I suppose." Meg was in such an agony of impatience that her voice grated irritably. "And Copernicus. But what about Father? Please, what about Father?"

"Wee aarre ggoingg tto yourr ffatherr," Mrs. Which said.

"But where is he?" Meg went over to Mrs. Which and stamped as though she were as young as Charles Wallace.

Mrs. Whatsit answered in a voice that was low but quite firm. "On a planet that has given in. So you must prepare to be very strong."

All traces of cheer had left the Happy Medium's face. She sat holding the great ball, looking down at the shadowed earth, and a slow tear coursed down her cheek. "I can't stand it any longer," she sobbed. "Watch now, children, watch!"

Chapter 6

THE HAPPY MEDIUM

Again they focused their eyes on the crystal ball. The earth with its fearful covering of dark shadow swam out of view and they moved rapidly through the Milky Way. And there was the Thing again.

"Watch!" the Medium told them.

The Darkness seemed to seethe and writhe. Was this meant to *comfort* them?

Suddenly there was a great burst of light through the Darkness. The light spread out and where it touched the Darkness the Darkness disappeared. The light spread until the patch of Dark Thing had vanished, and there was only a gentle shining, and through the shining came the stars, clear and pure. Then, slowly, the shining dwindled until it, too, was gone, and there was nothing but stars and starlight. No shadows. No fear. Only the stars and the clear darkness of space, quite different from the fearful darkness of the Thing.

"You see!" the Medium cried, smiling happily. "It can be overcome! It is being overcome all the time!"

Mrs. Whatsit sighed, a sigh so sad that Meg wanted to put her arms around her and comfort her.

"Tell us exactly what happened, then, please," Charles Wallace said in a small voice.

"It was a star," Mrs. Whatsit said sadly. "A star giving up its life in battle with the Thing. It won, oh, yes, my children, it won. But it lost its life in the winning."

Mrs. Which spoke again. Her voice sounded tired, and they knew that speaking was a tremendous effort for her. "Itt wass nnott sso llongg aggo fforr yyou, wwass itt?" she asked gently.

Mrs. Whatsit shook her head.

Charles Wallace went up to Mrs. Whatsit. "I see. Now I understand. You were a star, once, weren't you?"

Mrs. Whatsit covered her face with her hands as though she were embarrassed, and nodded.

"And you did—you did what that star just did?"

With her face still covered, Mrs. Whatsit nodded again.

Charles Wallace looked at her, very solemnly. "I should like to kiss you."

Mrs. Whatsit took her hands down from her face and pulled Charles Wallace to her in a quick embrace. He put his arms about her neck, pressed his cheek against hers, and then kissed her.

Meg felt that she would have liked to kiss Mrs. Whatsit, too, but that after Charles Wallace, anything that she or Calvin did or said would be anticlimax. She contented herself with looking at Mrs. Whatsit. Even though she was used to Mrs. Whatsit's odd getup (and the very oddness of it was what made her seem so comforting), she realized with a fresh shock that it was not Mrs. Whatsit herself that she was seeing at all. The complete, the true Mrs. Whatsit, Meg realized, was beyond human understanding. What she saw was only the game Mrs. Whatsit was playing; it was an amusing and charming game, a game full of both laughter and comfort, but it was only the tiniest facet of all the things Mrs. Whatsit *could* be.

"I didn't mean to tell you," Mrs. Whatsit faltered. "I didn't mean ever to let you know. But, oh, my dears, I did so love being a star!"

"Yyouu arre sstill verry yyoungg," Mrs. Which said, her voice faintly chiding.

The Medium sat looking happily at the star-filled sky in her ball, smiling and nodding and chuckling gently. But Meg noticed that her eyes were drooping, and suddenly her head fell forward and she gave a faint snore.

"Poor thing," Mrs. Whatsit said, "we've worn her out. It's very hard work for her."

"Please, Mrs. Whatsit," Meg asked, "what happens now? Why are we here? What do we do next? Where is Father? When are we going to him?" She clasped her hands pleadingly.

"One thing at a time, love!" Mrs. Whatsit said.

Mrs. Who cut in. *"As paredes tem ouvidos.* That's Portuguese. *Walls have ears."*

"Yes, let us go outside," Mrs. Whatsit said. "Come, we'll let her sleep."

But as they turned to go, the Medium jerked her head up and smiled at them radiantly. "You weren't going to go without saying goodbye to me, were you?" she asked.

"We thought we'd just let you sleep, dear." Mrs. Whatsit patted the Medium's shoulder. "We worked you terribly hard and we know you must be very tired."

"But I was going to give you some ambrosia or nectar or at least some tea—"

At this Meg realized that she was hungry. How much time had passed since they had had their bowls of stew? she wondered.

But Mrs. Whatsit said, "Oh, thank you, dear, but I think we'd better be going."

"*They* don't need to eat, you know," Charles Wallace whispered to Meg. "At least not food, the way we do. Eating's just a game with them. As soon as we get organized again I'd better remind them that they'll have to feed us sooner or later."

The Medium smiled and nodded. "It does seem as though I should be able to do something *nice* for you, after having had to show those poor children such horrid things. Would they like to see their mother before they go?"

"Could we see Father?" Meg asked eagerly.

"Nno," Mrs. Which said. "Wwee aare ggoingg tto yourr ffatherr, Mmegg. Doo nnott bbee immpatientt."

"But she *could* see her mother, couldn't she?" the Medium wheedled.

"Oh, why not," Mrs. Whatsit put in. "It won't take long and it can't do any harm."

"And Calvin, too?" Meg asked. "Could he see his mother, too?"

Calvin touched Meg in a quick gesture, and whether it was of thanks or apprehension she was not sure.

"I tthinkk itt iss a misstake." Mrs. Which was disapproving. "Bbutt ssince yyou hhave menttionedd itt I ssupposse yyouu musstt ggo aheadd."

"I hate it when she gets cross," Mrs. Whatsit said, glancing over at Mrs. Which, "and the trouble is, she always seems to be right. But I really don't see how it could hurt, and it might make you all feel better. Go on, Medium dear."

The Medium, smiling and humming softly, turned the crystal ball a little between her hands. Stars, comets, planets, flashed across the sky, and then the earth came into view again, the darkened earth, closer, closer, till it filled the globe, and they had somehow gone through the darkness until the soft white of clouds and the gentle outline of continents shone clearly.

"Calvin's mother first," Meg whispered to the Medium.

The globe became hazy, cloudy, then shadows began to solidify, to clarify, and they were looking into an untidy kitchen with a sink full of unwashed dishes. In front of the sink stood an unkempt woman with gray hair stringing about her face. Her mouth was open and Meg could see the toothless gums and it seemed that she could almost hear her screaming at two small children who were standing by her. Then she grabbed a long wooden spoon from the sink and began whacking one of the children.

"Oh, dear—" the Medium murmured, and the picture began to dissolve. "I didn't really—"

"It's all right," Calvin said in a low voice. "I think I'd rather you knew."

Now instead of reaching out to Calvin for safety, Meg took his hand in hers, not saying anything in words but trying to tell him by the pressure of her fingers what she felt. If anyone had told her only the day before that she, Meg, the snaggle-toothed, the myopic, the clumsy, would be taking a boy's hand to offer him comfort and strength, particularly a popular and important boy like Calvin, the idea would have been beyond her comprehension. But now it seemed as natural to want to help and protect Calvin as it did Charles Wallace.

The shadows were swirling in the crystal again, and as they cleared Meg began to recognize her mother's lab at home. Mrs. Murry was sitting perched on her high stool, writing away at a sheet of paper on a clipboard on her lap. She's writing Father, Meg thought. The way she always does. Every night.

The tears that she could never learn to control swam to her eyes as she watched. Mrs. Murry looked up from her letter, almost as though she were looking toward the children, and then her head drooped and she put it down on the paper, and sat there, huddled up, letting herself relax into an unhappiness that she never allowed her children to see.

And now the desire for tears left Meg. The hot, protective anger she had felt for Calvin when she looked into his home she now felt turned toward her mother.

"Let's go!" she cried harshly. "Let's *do* something!"

"She's always so right," Mrs. Whatsit murmured, looking towards Mrs. Which. "Sometimes I wish she'd just say I told you so and have done with it."

"I only meant to help—" the Medium wailed.

"Oh, Medium, dear, *don't* feel badly," Mrs. Whatsit said swiftly. "Look at something cheerful, do. I can't bear to have you distressed!"

"It's all right," Meg assured the Medium earnestly. "Truly it is, Mrs. Medium, and we thank you very much."

"Are you sure?" the Medium asked, brightening.

"Of course! It really helped ever so much because it made me mad, and when I'm mad I don't have room to be scared."

"Well, kiss me goodbye for good luck, then," the Medium said.

Meg went over to her and gave her a quick kiss, and so did Charles Wallace. The Medium looked smilingly at Calvin, and winked. "I want the young man to kiss me, too. I always did love red hair. And it'll give you good luck, Laddie-me-love."

Calvin bent down, blushing, and awkwardly kissed her cheek.

The Medium tweaked his nose. "You've got a lot to learn, my boy," she told him.

"Now, goodbye, Medium dear, and many thanks," Mrs. Whatsit said. "I dare say we'll see you in an eon or two."

"Where are you going in case I want to tune in?" the Medium asked.

"Camazotz," Mrs. Whatsit told her. (Where and what was Camazotz? Meg did not like the sound of the word or the way in which Mrs. Whatsit pronounced it.) "But please don't distress yourself on our behalf. You know you don't like looking in on the dark planets, and it's very upsetting to us when you aren't happy."

"But I must know what happens to the children," the Medium said. "It's my worst trouble, getting fond. If I didn't get fond I could be happy all the time. *Oh,* well, *ho* hum, I manage to keep pretty jolly, and a little snooze will do wonders for me right now. Goodbye, everyb—" and her word got lost in the general b-b-bz-z of a snore.

"Ccome," Mrs. Which ordered, and they followed her out of the darkness of the cave to the impersonal grayness of the Medium's planet.

"Nnoww, cchilldrenn, yyouu musstt nott bee frrightennedd att whatt iss ggoingg tto hhappenn," Mrs. Which warned.

"Stay angry, little Meg," Mrs. Whatsit whispered. "You will need all your anger now."

Without warning Meg was swept into nothingness again. This time the nothingness was interrupted by a feeling of clammy coldness such as she had never felt before. The coldness deepened and swirled all about her and through her, and was filled with a new and strange kind of darkness that was a completely tangible thing, a thing that wanted to eat and digest her like some enormous malignant beast of prey.

Then the darkness was gone. Had it been the shadow, the Black Thing? Had they had to travel through it to get to her father?

There was the by-now-familiar tingling in her hands and feet and the push through hardness, and she was on her feet, breathless but unharmed, standing beside Calvin and Charles Wallace.

"Is this Camazotz?" Charles Wallace asked as Mrs. Whatsit materialized in front of him.

"Yes," she answered. "Now let us just stand and get our breath and look around."

They were standing on a hill and as Meg looked about her she felt that it could easily be a hill on earth. There were the familiar trees she knew so well at home: birches, pines, maples. And though it was warmer than it had been when they so precipitously left the apple orchard, there was a faintly autumnal touch to the air; near them were several small trees with reddened leaves very like sumac, and a big patch of goldenrod-like flowers. As she looked down the hill she could see the smokestacks of a town, and it might have been one of any number of familiar towns. There seemed to be nothing strange, or different, or frightening, in the landscape.

But Mrs. Whatsit came to her and put an arm around her comfortingly. "I can't stay with you here, you know, love," she said. "You three children will be on your own. We will be near you; we will be watching you. But you will not be able to see us or to ask us for help, and we will not be able to come to you."

"But is Father here?" Meg asked tremblingly.

"Yes."

"But where? When will we see him?" She was poised for running, as though she were going to sprint off, immediately, to wherever her father was.

"That I cannot tell you. You will just have to wait until the propitious moment."

Charles Wallace looked steadily at Mrs. Whatsit. "Are you afraid for us?"

"A little."

"But if you weren't afraid to do what you did when you were a star, why should you be afraid for us now?"

"But I was afraid," Mrs. Whatsit said gently. She looked steadily at each of the three children in turn. "You will need help," she told them, "but all I am allowed to give you is a little talisman. Calvin, your great gift is your ability to communicate, to communicate with all kinds of people. So, for you, I will strengthen this gift. Meg, I give you your faults."

"My faults!" Meg cried.

"Your faults."

"But I'm always trying to get rid of my faults!"

"Yes," Mrs. Whatsit said. "However, I think you'll find they'll come in very handy on Camazotz. Charles Wallace, to you I can give only the resilience of your childhood."

From somewhere Mrs. Who's glasses glimmered and they heard her voice. "Calvin," she said, "a hint. For you a hint. Listen well:

> . . . For that he was a spirit too delicate
> To act their earthly and abhorr'd commands,
> Refusing their grand hests, they did confine him
> By help of their most potent ministers,
> And in their most unmitigable rage,
> Into a cloven pine; within which rift
> Imprisoned, he didst painfully remain. . . .

Shakespeare. *The Tempest*."

"Where are you, Mrs. Who?" Charles Wallace asked. "Where is Mrs. Which?"

"We cannot come to you now," Mrs. Who's voice blew to them like the wind. *"Allwissend bin ich nicht; doch viel ist mir bewisst.* Goethe. *I do not know everything; still many things I understand.* That is for you, Charles. Remember that you do not know everything." Then the voice was directed to Meg. "To you I leave my glasses, little blind-as-a-bat. But do not use them except as a last resort. Save them for the final moment of peril." As she spoke there was another shimmer of spectacles, and then it was gone, and the voice faded out with it. The spectacles were in Meg's hand. She put them carefully into the breast pocket of her blazer, and the knowledge that they were there somehow made her a little less afraid.

"Tto alll tthreee off yyou I ggive mmy ccommandd," Mrs. Which said. "Ggo ddownn inntoo tthee ttownn. Ggo ttogetherr. Ddoo nnott llett tthemm ssepparate yyou. Bbee sstrongg." There was a flicker and then it vanished. Meg shivered.

Mrs. Whatsit must have seen the shiver, for she patted Meg on the shoulder. Then she turned to Calvin. "Take care of Meg."

"I can take care of Meg," Charles Wallace said rather sharply. "I always have."

Mrs. Whatsit looked at Charles Wallace, and the creaky voice seemed somehow both to soften and to deepen at the same time. "Charles Wallace, the danger here is greatest for you."

"Why?"

"Because of what you are. Just exactly because of what you are you will be by far the most vulnerable. You *must* stay with Meg and Calvin. You must *not* go off on your own. Beware of pride and arrogance, Charles, for they may betray you."

At the tone of Mrs. Whatsit's voice, both warning

and frightening, Meg shivered again. And Charles Wallace butted up against Mrs. Whatsit in the way he often did with his mother, whispering, "Now I think I know what you meant about being afraid."

"Only a fool is not afraid," Mrs. Whatsit told him. "Now go." And where she had been there was only sky and grasses and a small rock.

"Come *on*," Meg said impatiently. "Come on, let's *go!*" She was completely unaware that her voice was trembling like an aspen leaf. She took Charles Wallace and Calvin each by the hand and started down the hill.

Below them the town was laid out in harsh angular patterns. The houses in the outskirts were all exactly alike, small square boxes painted gray. Each had a small, rectangular plot of lawn in front, with a straight line of dull-looking flowers edging the path to the door. Meg had a feeling that if she could count the flowers there would be exactly the same number for each house. In front of all the houses children were playing. Some were skipping rope, some were bouncing balls. Meg felt vaguely that something was wrong with their play. It seemed exactly like children playing around any housing development at home, and yet there was something different about it. She looked at Calvin, and saw that he, too, was puzzled.

"Look!" Charles Wallace said suddenly. "They're skipping and bouncing in rhythm! Everyone's doing it at exactly the same moment."

This was so. As the skipping rope hit the pavement, so did the ball. As the rope curved over the head of the jumping child, the child with the ball caught the ball. Down came the ropes. Down came the balls. Over and over again. Up. Down. All in rhythm. All identical. Like the houses. Like the paths. Like the flowers.

Then the doors of all the houses opened simultaneously, and out came women like a row of paper dolls. The print of their dresses was different, but they all gave the appearance of being the same. Each woman stood on the steps of her house. Each clapped. Each child with the ball caught the ball. Each child with the skipping rope folded the rope. Each child turned and walked into the house. The doors clicked shut behind them.

"How can they do it?" Meg asked wonderingly. "We couldn't do it that way if we tried. What does it mean?"

"Let's go back." Calvin's voice was urgent.

"Back?" Charles Wallace asked. "Where?"

"I don't know. Anywhere. Back to the hill. Back to Mrs. Whatsit and Mrs. Who and Mrs. Which. I don't like this."

"But they aren't there. Do you think they'd come to us if we turned back now?"

"I don't like it," Calvin said again.

"Come *on.*" Impatience made Meg squeak. "You *know* we can't go back. Mrs. Whatsit said to go into the town." She started on down the street, and the two boys followed her. The houses, all identical, continued, as far as the eye could reach.

Then, all at once, they saw the same thing, and stopped to watch. In front of one of the houses stood a little boy with a ball, and he was bouncing it. But he bounced it rather badly and with no particular rhythm, sometimes dropping it and running after it with awkward, furtive leaps, sometimes throwing it up into the air and trying to catch it. The door of his house opened and out ran one of the mother figures. She looked wildly up and down the street, saw the children and put her hand to her mouth as though to stifle a scream, grabbed the little boy and rushed indoors with him. The ball dropped from his fingers and rolled out into the street.

Charles Wallace ran after it and picked it up, holding it out for Meg and Calvin to see. It seemed like a perfectly ordinary, brown rubber ball.

"Let's take it in to him and see what happens," Charles Wallace suggested.

Meg pulled at him. "Mrs. Whatsit said for us to go on into the town."

"Well, we *are* in the town, aren't we? The outskirts anyhow. I want to know more about this. I have a hunch it may help us later. You go on if you don't want to come with me."

"No," Calvin said firmly. "We're going to stay together. Mrs. Whatsit said we weren't to let them separate us. But I'm with you on this. Let's knock and see what happens."

They went up the path to the house, Meg reluctant, eager to get on into the town. "Let's hurry," she begged, *"please!* Don't you want to find Father?"

"Yes," Charles Wallace said, "but not blindly. How can we help him if we don't know what we're up against? And it's obvious we've been brought here to help him, not just to find him." He walked briskly up the steps and knocked at the door. They waited. Nothing happened. Then Charles Wallace saw a bell, and this he rang. They could hear the bell buzzing in the house, and the sound of it echoed down the street. After a moment the mother figure opened the door. All up and down the street other doors opened, but only a crack, and eyes peered toward the three children and the woman looking fearfully out the door at them.

"What do you want?" she asked. "It isn't paper

time yet; we've had milk time; we've had this month's Puller Prush Person; and I've given my Decency Donations regularly. All my papers are in order."

"I think your little boy dropped his ball," Charles Wallace said, holding it out.

The woman pushed the ball away. "Oh, no! The children in our section *never* drop balls! They're all perfectly trained. We haven't had an Aberration for three years."

All up and down the block, heads nodded in agreement.

Charles Wallace moved closer to the woman and looked past her into the house. Behind her in the shadows he could see the little boy, who must have been about his own age.

"You can't come in," the woman said. "You haven't shown me any papers. I don't have to let you in if you haven't any papers."

Charles Wallace held the ball out beyond the woman so that the little boy could see it. Quick as a flash the boy leaped forward and grabbed the ball from Charles Wallace's hand, then darted back into the shadows. The woman went very white, opened her mouth as though to say something, then slammed the door in their faces instead. All up and down the street doors slammed.

"What are they afraid of?" Charles Wallace asked. "What's the matter with them?"

"Don't *you* know?" Meg asked him. "Don't you know what all this is about, Charles?"

"Not yet," Charles Wallace said. "Not even an inkling. And I'm trying. But I didn't get through anywhere. Not even a chink. Let's go." He stumped down the steps.

After several blocks the houses gave way to apartment buildings; at least Meg felt sure that that was what they must be. They were fairly tall, rectangular buildings, absolutely plain, each window, each entrance exactly like every other. Then, coming toward them down the street, was a boy about Calvin's age riding a machine that was something like a combination of a bicycle and a motorcycle. It had the slimness and lightness of a bicycle, and yet as the foot pedals turned they seemed to generate an unseen source of power, so that the boy could pedal very slowly and yet move along the street quite swiftly. As he reached each entrance he thrust one hand into a bag he wore slung over his shoulder, pulled out a roll of papers, and tossed it into the entrance. It might have been Dennys or Sandy or any one of hundreds of boys with a newspaper route in any one of hundreds of towns back home, and yet, as with the children playing ball and jumping rope, there was something wrong about it. The rhythm of the gesture never varied. The paper flew in identically the same arc at each doorway, landed in identically the same spot. It was impossible for anybody to throw with such consistent perfection.

Calvin whistled. "I wonder if they play baseball here?"

As the boy saw them he slowed down on his machine and stopped, his hand arrested as it was about to plunge into the paper bag. "What are you kids doing out on the street?" he demanded. "Only route boys are allowed out now, you know that."

"No, we don't know it," Charles Wallace said. "We're strangers here. How about telling us something about this place?"

"You mean you've had your entrance papers processed and everything?" the boy asked. "You must have if you're here," he answered himself.

"And what are you doing here if you don't know about us?"

"You tell me," Charles Wallace said.

"Are you examiners?" the boy asked a little anxiously. "Everybody knows our city has the best Central Intelligence Center on the planet. Our production levels are the highest. Our factories never close; our machines never stop rolling. Added to this we have five poets, one musician, three artists, and six sculptors, all perfectly channeled."

"What are you quoting from?" Charles Wallace asked.

"The Manual, of course," the boy said. "We are the most oriented city on the planet. There has been no trouble of any kind for centuries. All Camazotz knows our record. That is why we are the capital city of Camazotz. That is why CENTRAL Central Intelligence is located here. That is why IT makes ITs home here." There was something about the way he said "IT" that made a shiver run up and down Meg's spine.

But Charles Wallace asked briskly, "Where is this Central Intelligence Center of yours?"

"CENTRAL Central," the boy corrected. "Just keep going and you can't miss it. You *are* strangers, aren't you! What are you doing here?"

"Are you supposed to ask questions?" Charles Wallace demanded severely.

The boy went white, just as the woman had. "I humbly beg your pardon. I must continue my route now or I will have to talk my timing into the explainer." And he shot off down the street on his machine.

Charles Wallace stared after him. "What is it?" he asked Meg and Charles. "There was something funny about the way he talked, as though—well, as though he weren't really doing the talking. Know what I mean?"

Calvin nodded, thoughtfully. "Funny is right. Funny peculiar. Not only the way he talked, either. The whole thing smells."

"Come *on.*" Meg pulled at them. How many times was it she had urged them on? "Let's go find Father. He'll be able to explain it all to us."

They walked on. After several more blocks they began to see other people, grown-up people, not children walking up and down and across the streets. These people ignored the children entirely, seeming to be completely intent on their own business. Some of them went into the apartment buildings. Most of them were heading in the same direction as the children. As these people came to the main street from the side streets they would swing around the corners with an odd, automatic stride, as though they were so deep in their own problems and the route was so familiar that they didn't have to pay any attention to where they were going.

After a while the apartment buildings gave way to what must have been office buildings, great stern structures with enormous entrances. Men and women with brief cases poured in and out.

Charles Wallace went up to one of the women, saying politely, "Excuse me, but could you please tell me—" But she hardly glanced at him as she continued on her way.

"Look." Meg pointed. Ahead of them, across a square, was the largest building they had ever seen, higher than the Empire State Building, and almost as long as it was high.

"This must be it," Charles Wallace said, "their CENTRAL Central Intelligence or whatever it is. Let's go on."

"But if Father's in some kind of trouble with this planet," Meg objected, "isn't that exactly where we *shouldn't* go?"

"Well, how do you propose finding him?" Charles Wallace demanded.

"I certainly wouldn't ask *there!*"

"I didn't say anything about asking. But we aren't going to have the faintest idea where or how to begin to look for him until we find out something more about this place, and I have a hunch that that's the place to start. If you have a better idea, Meg, why of course just say so."

"Oh, get down off your high horse," Meg said crossly. "Let's go to your old CENTRAL Central Intelligence and get it over with."

"I think we ought to have passports or something," Calvin suggested. "This is much more than leaving America to go to Europe. And that boy and the woman both seemed to care so much about having things in proper order. We certainly haven't got any papers in proper order."

"If we needed passports or papers Mrs. Whatsit would have told us so," Charles Wallace said.

Calvin put his hands on his hips and looked down at Charles Wallace. "Now look here, old sport. I love those three old girls just as much as you do, but I'm not sure they know *everything.*"

"They know a lot more than we do."

"Granted. But you know Mrs. Whatsit talked about having been a star. I wouldn't think that being a star would give her much practice in knowing about people. When she tried to be a person she came pretty close to goofing it up. There was never anybody on land or sea like Mrs. Whatsit the way she got herself up."

"She was just having fun," Charles said. "If she'd

wanted to look like you or Meg I'm sure she could have."

Calvin shook his head. "I'm not so sure. And these people seem to be *people,* if you know what I mean. They aren't like us, I grant you that, there's something very off-beat about them. But they're lots more like ordinary people than the ones on Uriel."

"Do you suppose they're robots?" Meg suggested.

Charles Wallace shook his head. "No. That boy who dropped the ball wasn't any robot. And I don't think the rest of them are, either. Let me listen for a minute."

They stood very still, side by side, in the shadow of one of the big office buildings. Six large doors kept swinging open, shut, open, shut, as people went in and out, in and out, looking straight ahead, straight ahead, paying no attention to the children whatsoever, whatsoever. Charles wore his listening, probing look. "They're not robots," he said suddenly and definitely. "I'm not sure *what* they are, but they're not robots. I can feel minds there. I can't get at them at all, but I can feel them sort of pulsing. Let me try a minute more."

The three of them stood there very quietly. The doors kept opening and shutting, opening and shutting, and the stiff people hurried in and out, in and out, walking jerkily like figures in an old silent movie. Then, abruptly, the stream of movement thinned. There were only a few people and these moved more rapidly, as if the film had been speeded up. One white-faced man in a dark suit looked directly at the children, said, "Oh, dear, I shall be late," and flickered into the building.

"He's like the white rabbit," Meg giggled nervously.

"I'm scared," Charles said. "I can't reach them at all. I'm completely shut out."

"We have to find Father—" Meg started again.

"Meg—" Charles Wallace's eyes were wide and frightened. "I'm not sure I'll even know Father. It's been so long, and I was only a baby—"

Meg's reassurance came quickly. "You'll know him! Of course you'll know him! The way you'd know me even without looking because I'm always there for you, you can always reach in—"

"Yes." Charles punched one small fist into an open palm with a gesture of great decision. "Let's go to CENTRAL Central Intelligence."

Calvin reached out and caught both Charles and Meg by the arm. "You remember when we met, you asked me why I was there? And I told you it was because I had a compulsion, a feeling I just had to come to that particular place at that particular moment?"

"Yes, sure."

"I've got another feeling. Not the same kind, a different one, a feeling that if we go into that building we're going into terrible danger."

Chapter 7

THE MAN WITH RED EYES

"We knew we were going to be in danger," Charles Wallace said. "Mrs. Whatsit told us that."

"Yes, and she told us that it was going to be worse for you than for Meg and me, and that you must be careful. You stay right here with Meg, old sport, and let me go in and case the joint and then report to you."

"No," Charles Wallace said firmly. "She told us to stay together. She told us not to go off by ourselves."

"She told *you* not to go off by yourself. I'm the oldest and I should go in first."

"No." Meg's voice was flat. "Charles is right, Cal. We have to stay together. Suppose you didn't come out and we had to go in after you? Unh-unh. Come on. But let's hold hands if you don't mind."

Holding hands, they crossed the square. The huge CENTRAL Central Intelligence Building had only one door, but it was an enormous one, at least two stories high and wider than a room, made of a dull, bronze-like material.

"Do we just knock?" Meg giggled.

Calvin studied the door. "There isn't any handle or knob or latch or anything. Maybe there's another way to get in."

"Let's try knocking anyhow," Charles said. He raised his hand, but before he touched the door it slid up from the top and to each side, splitting into three sections that had been completely invisible a moment before. The startled children looked into a great entrance hall of dull, greeny marble. Marble benches lined three of the walls. People were sitting there like statues. The green of the marble reflecting on their faces made them look bilious. They turned their heads as the door opened, saw the children, looked away again.

"Come on," Charles said, and, still holding hands, they stepped in. As they crossed the threshold the door shut silently behind them. Meg looked at Calvin and Charles and they, like the waiting people, were a sickly green.

The children went up to the blank fourth wall. It seemed unsubstantial, as though one might almost be able to walk through it. Charles put out his hand. "It's solid, and icy cold."

Calvin touched it, too. "Ugh."

Meg's left hand was held by Charles, her right by Calvin, and she had no desire to let go of either of them to touch the wall.

"Let's ask somebody something." Charles led them over to one of the benches. "Er, could you tell us what's the procedure around here?" he asked one of the men. The men all wore nondescript business suits, and though their features were as different one from the other as the features of men on earth, there was also a sameness to them.

—Like the sameness of people riding in a subway, Meg thought. —Only on a subway every once in a while there's somebody different and here there isn't.

The man looked at the children warily. "The procedure for what?"

"How do we see whoever's in authority?" Charles asked.

"You present your papers to the A machine. You ought to know that," the man said severely.

"Where is the A machine?" Calvin asked.

The man pointed to the blank wall.

"But there isn't a door or anything," Calvin said. "How do we get in?"

"You put your S papers in the B slot," the man said. "Why are you asking me these stupid questions? Do you think I don't know the answers? You'd better not play any games around here or you'll have to go through the Process machine again and you don't want to do *that*."

"We're strangers here," Calvin said. "That's why we don't know about things. Please tell us, sir, who you are and what you do."

"I run a number-one spelling machine on the second-grade level."

"But what are you doing here now?" Charles Wallace asked.

"I am here to report that one of my letters is jamming, and until it can be properly oiled by an F Grade oiler there is danger of jammed minds."

"Strawberry jam or raspberry?" Charles Wallace murmured. Calvin looked down at Charles and shook his head warningly. Meg gave the little boy's hand a slight, understanding pressure. Charles Wallace, she was quite sure, was not trying to be rude or funny; it was his way of whistling in the dark.

The man looked at Charles sharply. "I think I shall have to report you. I'm fond of children, due to the nature of my work and I don't like to get them in trouble, but rather than run the risk myself of reprocessing I must report you."

"Maybe that's a good idea," Charles said. "Who do you report us to?"

"To *whom* do I report you."

"Well, to whom, then. I'm not on the second-grade level yet."

—I wish he wouldn't act so sure of himself, Meg thought, looking anxiously at Charles and holding his hand more and more tightly until he wriggled his fingers in protest. That's what Mrs. Whatsit said he had to watch, being proud. —Don't, please don't, she thought hard at Charles Wallace. She wondered if Calvin realized that a lot of the arrogance was bravado.

The man stood up, moving jerkily as though he had been sitting for a long time. "I hope he isn't too hard on you," he murmured as he led the children toward the empty fourth wall. "But I've been reprocessed once and that was more than enough. And I don't want to get sent to IT. I've never been sent to IT and I can't risk having that happen."

There was IT again. What was this IT?

The man took from his pocket a folder filled with papers of every color. He shuffled through them carefully, finally withdrawing one. "I've had several reports to make lately. I shall have to ask for a requisition for more A-21 cards. "He took the card and put it against the wall. It slid through the marble, as though it were being sucked in, and disappeared. "You may be detained for a few days," the man said, "but I'm sure they won't be too hard on you because of your youth. Just relax and don't fight and it will all be much easier for you." He went back to his seat, leaving the children standing and staring at the blank wall.

And suddenly the wall was no longer there and they were looking into an enormous room lined with machines. They were not unlike the great computing machines Meg had seen in her science books and that she knew her father sometimes worked with. Some did not seem to be in use; in others lights were flickering on and off. In one machine a long tape was being eaten; in another a series of dot-dashes were being punched. Several white-robed attendants were moving about, tending the machines. If they saw the children they gave no sign.

Calvin muttered something.

"What?" Meg asked him.

"There is nothing to fear except fear itself," Calvin said. "I'm quoting. Like Mrs. Who. Meg, I'm scared stiff."

"So 'm I." Meg held his hand more tightly. "Come on."

They stepped into the room with the machines. In spite of the enormous width of the room it was even longer than it was wide. Perspective made the long rows of machines seem almost to meet. The children walked down the center of the room, keeping as far from the machines as possible.

"Though I don't suppose they're radioactive or anything," Charles Wallace said, "or that they're going to reach out and grab us and chew us up."

After they had walked for what seemed like miles, they could see that the enormous room did have an end, and that at the end there was something.

Charles Wallace said suddenly, and his voice held panic, "Don't let go of my hands! Hold me tight! He's trying to get at me!"

"Who?" Meg squeaked.

"I don't know. But he's trying to get in at me! I can feel him!"

"Let's go back." Calvin started to pull away.

"No," Charles Wallace said. "I have to go on. We have to make decisions, and we can't make them if they're based on fear." His voice sounded old and strange and remote. Meg, clasping his small hand tightly, could feel it sweating in hers.

As they approached the end of the room their steps slowed. Before them was a platform. On the platform was a chair, and on the chair was a man.

What was there about him that seemed to contain all the coldness and darkness they had felt as they plunged through the Black Thing on their way to this planet?

"I have been waiting for you, my dears," the man said. His voice was kind and gentle, not at all the cold and frightening voice Meg had expected. It took her a moment to realize that though the voice came from the man, he had not opened his mouth or moved his lips at all, that no real words had been spoken to fall upon her ears, that he had somehow communicated directly into their brains.

"But how does it happen that there are three of you?" the man asked.

Charles Wallace spoke with harsh boldness, but Meg could feel him trembling. "Oh, Calvin just came along for the ride."

"Oh, he did, did he?" For a moment there was a sharpness to the voice that spoke inside their minds. Then it relaxed and became soothing again. "I hope that it has been a pleasant one so far."

"Very educational," Charles Wallace said.

"Let Calvin speak for himself," the man ordered.

Calvin growled, his lips tight, his body rigid. "I have nothing to say."

Meg stared at the man in horrified fascination. His eyes were bright and had a reddish glow. Above his head was a light, and it glowed in the same manner as the eyes, pulsing, throbbing, in steady rhythm.

Charles Wallace shut his eyes tightly. "Close your eyes," he said to Meg and Calvin. "Don't look at the light. Don't look at his eyes. He'll hypnotize you."

"Clever, aren't you? Focusing your eyes would, of course, help," the soothing voice went on, "but there are other ways, my little man. Oh, yes, there are other ways."

"If you try it on me I shall kick you!" Charles Wallace said. It was the first time Meg had ever heard Charles Wallace suggesting violence.

"Oh, will you, indeed, my little man?" The thought was tolerant, amused, but four men in dark smocks appeared and flanked the children.

"Now, my dears," the words continued, "I shall of course have no need of recourse to violence, but I thought perhaps it would save you pain if I showed you at once that it would do you no good to try to oppose me. You see, what you will soon realize is that there is no need to fight me. Not only is there no need, but you will not have the slightest desire to do so. For why should you wish to fight someone who is here only to save you pain and trouble? For you, as well as for the rest of all the happy, useful people on this planet, *I,* in my own strength, am willing to assume all the pain, all the responsibility, all the burdens of thought and decision."

"We will make our own decisions, thank you," Charles Wallace said.

"But of *course.* And our decisions will be one, yours and mine. Don't you see how much better, how much *easier* for you that is? Let me show you. Let us say the multiplication table together."

"No," Charles Wallace said.

"Once one is one. Once two is two. Once three is three."

"Mary had a little lamb!" Charles Wallace shouted. "Its fleece was white as snow!"

"Once four is four. Once five is five. Once six is six."

"And everywhere that Mary went the lamb was sure to go!"

"Once seven is seven. Once eight is eight. Once nine is nine."

"Peter, Peter, pumpkin eater, had a wife and couldn't keep her—"

"Once ten is ten. Once eleven is eleven. Once twelve is twelve."

The number words pounded insistently against Meg's brain. They seemed to be boring their way into her skull.

"Twice one is two. Twice two is four. Twice three is six."

Calvin's voice came out in an angry shout. "Fourscore and seven years ago our fathers brought forth on this continent a new nation, conceived in liberty, and dedicated to the proposition that all men are created equal."

"Twice four is eight. Twice five is ten. Twice six is twelve."

"Father!" Meg screamed. "Father!" The scream, half involuntary, jerked her mind back out of darkness.

The words of the multiplication table seemed to break up into laughter. "Splendid! Splendid! You have passed your preliminary tests with flying colors."

"You didn't think we were as easy as all that, falling for that old stuff, did you?" Charles Wallace demanded.

"Ah, I hoped not. I most sincerely hoped not. But after all you are very young and very impressionable, and the younger the better, my little man. The younger the better."

Meg looked up at the fiery eyes, at the light pulsing above them, and then away. She tried looking at the mouth, at the thin, almost colorless lips, and this was more possible, even though she had to look obliquely, so that she was not sure exactly what the face really looked like, whether it was young or old, cruel or kind, human or alien.

"If you please," she said, trying to sound calm and brave. "The only reason we are here is because we think our father is here. Can you tell us where to find him?"

"Ah, your father!" There seemed to be a great chortling of delight. "Ah, yes, your father! It is not *can* I, you know, young lady, but *will* I?"

"Will you, then?"

"That depends on a number of things. Why do you want your father?"

"Didn't you ever have a father yourself?" Meg demanded. "You don't want him for a *reason*. You want him because he's your *father*."

"Ah, but he hasn't been *acting* very like a father, lately, has he? Abandoning his wife and his four little children to go gallivanting off on wild adventures of his own."

"He was working for the government. He'd never have left us otherwise. And we want to see him, please. Right now."

"My, but the little miss is impatient! Patience, patience, young lady."

Meg did not tell the man on the chair that patience was not one of her virtues.

"And by the way, my children," he continued blandly, "you don't need to vocalize verbally with me, you know. I can understand you quite as well as you can understand me."

Charles Wallace put his hands on his hips defiantly. "The spoken word is one of the triumphs of man," he proclaimed, "and I intend to continue using it, particularly with people I don't trust." But his voice was shaking. Charles Wallace, who even as an infant had seldom cried, was near tears.

"And you don't trust me?"

"What reason have you given us to trust you?"

"What cause have I given you for *dis*trust?" The thin lips curled slightly.

Suddenly Charles Wallace darted forward and hit the man as hard as he could, which was fairly hard, as he had had a good deal of coaching from the twins.

"Charles!" Meg screamed.

The men in dark smocks moved smoothly but with swiftness to Charles. The man in the chair casually raised one finger, and the men dropped back.

"Hold it—" Calvin whispered, and together he and Meg darted forward and grabbed Charles Wallace, pulling him back from the platform.

The man gave a wince and the thought of his voice was a little breathless, as though Charles Wallace's punch had succeeded in winding him. "May I ask why you did that?"

"Because you aren't you," Charles Wallace said. "I'm not sure what you are, but you"—he pointed to the man on the chair—"aren't what's talking to us. I'm sorry if I hurt you. I didn't think you were real. I thought perhaps you were a robot, because I don't feel anything coming directly from you. I'm not sure where it's coming from, but it's coming *through* you. It isn't you."

"Pretty smart, aren't you?" the thought asked, and Meg had an uncomfortable feeling that she detected a snarl.

"It's not that I'm smart," Charles Wallace said, and again Meg could feel the palm of his hand sweating inside hers.

"Try to find out who I am, then," the thought probed.

"I have been trying," Charles Wallace said, his voice high and troubled.

"Look into my eyes. Look deep within them and I will tell you."

Charles Wallace looked quickly at Meg and Calvin, then said, as though to himself, "I have to," and focused his clear blue eyes on the red ones of the man in the chair. Meg looked not at the man but at her brother. After a moment it seemed that his eyes were no longer focusing. The pupils grew smaller and smaller, as though he were looking into an intensely bright light, until they seemed to close entirely, until his eyes were nothing but an opaque blue. He slipped his hands out of Meg's and Calvin's and started walking slowly toward the man on the chair.

"No!" Meg screamed. "No!"

But Charles Wallace continued his slow walk forward, and she knew that he had not heard her.

"No!" she screamed again, and ran after him. With her inefficient flying tackle she landed on him. She was so much larger than he that he fell sprawling, hitting his head a sharp crack against the marble floor. She knelt by him, sobbing. After a moment of lying there as though he had been knocked out by the blow, he opened his eyes, shook his head, and sat up. Slowly the pupils of his eyes dilated until they were back to normal, and the blood came back to his white cheeks.

The man on the chair spoke directly into Meg's mind, and now there was a distinct menace to the words. "I am not pleased," he said to her. "I could very easily lose patience with you, and that, for your information, young lady, would not be good for your father. If you have the slightest desire to see your father again, you had better cooperate."

Meg reacted as she sometimes reacted to Mr. Jenkins at school. She scowled down at the ground in sullen fury. "It might help if you gave us something to eat," she complained. "We're all starved. If you're going to be horrible to us you might as well give us full stomachs first."

Again the thoughts coming at her broke into laughter. "Isn't she the funny girl, though! It's lucky for you that you amuse me, my dear, or I shouldn't be so easy on you. The boys I find not nearly so diverting. Ah, well. Now, tell me, young lady, if I feed you will you stop interfering with me?"

"No," Meg said.

"Starvation does work wonders, of course," the man told her. "I hate to use such primitive methods on you, but of course you realize that you force them on me."

"I wouldn't eat your old food, anyhow." Meg was still all churned up and angry as though she were in Mr. Jenkins' office. "I wouldn't trust it."

"Of course our food, being synthetic, is not superior to your messes of beans and bacon and so forth, but I assure you that it's far more nourishing, and though it has no taste of its own, a slight conditioning is all that is necessary to give you the illusion that you are eating a roast turkey dinner."

"If I ate now I'd throw up, anyhow," Meg said.

Still holding Meg's and Calvin's hands, Charles Wallace stepped forward. "Okay, what next?" he asked the man on the chair. "We've had enough of these preliminaries. Let's get on with it."

"That's exactly what we were doing," the man said, "until your sister interfered by practically giving you a brain concussion. Shall we try again?"

"No!" Meg cried. "No, Charles. *Please.* Let me do it. Or Calvin."

"But it is only the little boy whose neurological system is complex enough. If you tried to conduct the necessary neurons your brains would explode."

"And Charles's wouldn't?"

"I think not."

"But there's a possibility?"

"There's always a possibility."

"Then he mustn't do it."

"I think you will have to grant him the right to make his own decisions."

But Meg, with the dogged tenacity that had so often caused her trouble, continued. "You mean Calvin and I can't know who you really are?"

"Oh, no, I didn't say that. You can't know it in the same way, nor is it as important to me to have you know. Ah, here we are!" From somewhere in the shadows appeared four more men in dark smocks carrying a table. It was covered with a white cloth, like the tables used by Room Service in hotels, and held a metal hot box containing something that smelled delicious, something that smelled like a turkey dinner.

There's something phoney in the whole setup, Meg thought. There is definitely something rotten in the state of Camazotz.

Again the thoughts seemed to break into laughter. "Of course it doesn't *really* smell, but isn't it as good as though it really did?"

"I don't smell anything," Charles Wallace said.

"I know, young man, and think how much you're missing. This will all taste to you as though you were eating sand. But I suggest that you force it down. I would rather not have your decisions come from the weakness of an empty stomach."

The table was set up in front of them, and the dark-smocked men heaped their plates with turkey and dressing and mashed potatoes and gravy and little green peas with big yellow blobs of butter melting in them and cranberries and sweet potatoes topped with gooey browned marshmallows and olives and celery and rosebud radishes and—

Meg felt her stomach rumbling loudly. The saliva came to her mouth.

"Oh, Jeeminy—" Calvin mumbled.

Chairs appeared and the four men who had provided the feast slid back into the shadows.

Charles Wallace freed his hands from Meg and Calvin and plunked himself down on one of the chairs.

"Come on," he said. "If it's poisoned it's poisoned, but I don't think it is."

Calvin sat down. Meg continued to stand indecisively.

Calvin took a bite. He chewed. He swallowed. He looked at Meg. "If this isn't real, it's the best imitation you'll ever get."

Charles Wallace took a bite, made a face, and spit out his mouthful. "It's unfair!" he shouted at the man.

Laughter again. "Go on, little fellow. Eat."

Meg sighed and sat. "I don't think we should eat this stuff, but if you're going to, I'd better, too." She took a mouthful. "It tastes all right. Try some of mine, Charles." She held out a forkful of turkey.

Charles Wallace took it, made another face, but managed to swallow. "Still tastes like sand," he said. He looked at the man. "Why?"

"You know perfectly well why. You've shut your mind entirely to me. The other two can't. I can get in through the chinks. Not all the way in, but enough to give them a turkey dinner. You see, I'm really just a kind, jolly old gentleman."

"Ha," Charles Wallace said.

The man lifted his lips into a smile, and his smile was the most horrible thing Meg had ever seen. "Why don't you trust me, Charles? Why don't you trust me enough to come in and find out what I am? I am peace and utter rest. I am freedom from all responsibility. To come in to me is the last difficult decision you need ever make."

"If I come in can I get out again?" Charles Wallace asked.

"But of course, if you want to. But I don't think you will want to."

"If I come—not to stay, you understand—just to find out about you, will you tell us where Father is?"

"Yes. That is a promise. And I don't make promises lightly."

"Can I speak to Meg and Calvin alone, without your listening in?"

"No."

Charles shrugged. "Listen," he said to Meg and Calvin. "I have to find out what he really is. You know that. I'm going to try to hold back. I'm going to try to keep part of myself out. You mustn't stop me this time, Meg."

"But you won't be able to, Charles! He's stronger than you are! You know that!"

"I have to try."

"But Mrs. Whatsit warned you!"

"I have to try. For Father, Meg. Please. I want—I want to know my father—" For a moment his lips trembled. Then he was back in control. "But it isn't only Father, Meg. You know that, now. It's the Black Thing. We have to do what Mrs. Which sent us to do."

"Calvin—" Meg begged.

But Calvin shook his head. "He's right, Meg. And we'll be with him, no matter what happens."

"But what's going to happen?" Meg cried.

Charles Wallace looked up at the man. "Okay," he said. "Let's go."

Now the red eyes and the light above seemed to bore into Charles, and again the pupils of the little boy's eyes contracted. When the final point of black was lost in blue he turned away from the red eyes, looked at Meg, and smiled sweetly, but the smile was not Charles Wallace's smile.

"Come on, Meg, eat this delicious food that has been prepared for us," he said.

Meg snatched Charles Wallace's plate and threw it on the floor, so that the dinner splashed about and the plate broke into fragments. "No!" She cried, her voice rising shrilly. "No! No! No!"

From the shadows came one of the dark-smocked men and put another plate in front of Charles Wallace, and he began to eat eagerly. "What's wrong, Meg?" Charles Wallace asked. "Why are you being so belligerent and uncooperative?" The voice was Charles Wallace's voice, and yet it was different, too, somehow flattened out, almost as a voice might have sounded on the two-dimensional planet.

Meg grabbed wildly at Calvin, shrieking, "That isn't Charles! Charles is gone!"

Chapter 8

THE TRANSPARENT COLUMN

Charles Wallace sat there tucking away turkey and dressing as though it were the most delicious thing he had ever tasted. He was dressed like Charles Wallace; he looked like Charles Wallace; he had the same sandy brown hair, the same face that had not yet lost its baby roundness. Only the eyes were different, for the black was still swallowed up in blue. But it was far more than this that made Meg feel that Charles Wallace was gone, that the little boy in his place was only a copy of Charles Wallace, only a doll.

She fought down a sob. "Where is he?" she demanded of the man with red eyes. "What have you done with him? Where is Charles Wallace?"

"But my dear child, you are hysterical," the man thought at her. "He is right there, before you, well and happy. Completely well and happy for the first time in his life. And he is finishing his dinner, which you also would be wise to do."

"You know it isn't Charles!" Meg shouted. "You've got him somehow."

"Hush, Meg. There's no use trying to talk to him," Calvin said, speaking in a low voice into her ear. "What we have to do is hold Charles Wallace tight. He's there, somewhere, underneath, and we mustn't let them take him away from us. Help me hold him, Meg. Don't lose control of yourself. Not now. You've got to help me hold Charles!" He took the little boy firmly by one arm.

Fighting down her hysteria, Meg took Charles's other arm and held it tightly.

"You're hurting me, Meg!" Charles said sharply. "Let me go!"

"No," Meg said grimly.

"We've been all wrong." Charles Wallace's voice, Meg thought, might have been a recording. There was a canned quality to it. "He isn't an enemy at all. He's our friend."

"Nuts," Calvin said rudely.

"You don't understand, Calvin," Charles Wallace said. "Mrs. Whatsit, Mrs. Who, and Mrs. Which have confused us. They're the ones who are really our enemies. We never should have trusted them for a minute." He spoke in his calmest, most reasonable voice, the voice which infuriated the twins. He seemed to be looking directly at Calvin as he spoke, and yet Meg was sure that the bland blue eyes could not see, and that someone, something else was looking at Calvin through Charles.

Now the cold, strange eyes turned to her. "Meg, let go. I will explain it all to you, but you must let go."

"No." Meg gritted her teeth. She did not release her grasp, and Charles Wallace began to pull away with a power that was not his own, and her own spindly strength was no match against it. "Calvin!" she gasped as Charles Wallace wrenched his arm from her and stood up.

Calvin the athlete, Calvin the boy who split firewood and brought it in for his mother, whose muscles were strong and controlled, let go Charles Wallace's wrist and tackled him as though he were a football. Meg, in her panic and rage, darted at the man on the chair, intending to hit him as Charles Wallace had done, but the black-smocked men were too quick for her, and one of them held her with her arms pinioned behind her back.

"Calvin, I advise you to let me go," came Charles Wallace's voice from under Calvin.

Calvin, his face screwed up with grim determination, did not relax his hold. The man with red eyes nodded and three of the men moved in on Calvin (at least it took three of them), pried him loose, and held him as Meg was being held.

"Mrs. Whatsit!" Meg called despairingly. "Oh, Mrs. Whatsit!"

But Mrs. Whatsit did not come.

"Meg," Charles Wallace said. "Meg, just listen to me."

"Okay, I'm listening."

"We've been all wrong, I told you; we haven't understood. We've been fighting our friend, and Father's friend."

"If Father tells me he's our friend maybe I'll believe it. Maybe. Unless he's got Father—under—under a spell, or whatever it is, like you."

"This isn't a fairy tale. Spells indeed," Charles Wallace said. "Meg, you've got to stop fighting and relax. Relax and be happy. Oh, Meg, if you'd just relax you'd realize that all our troubles are over. You don't understand what a wonderful place we've come to. You see, on this planet everything is in perfect order because everybody has learned to relax, to give in, to submit. All you have to do is look quietly and steadily into the eyes of our good friend here, for he is our friend, dear sister, and he will take you in as he has taken me."

"Taken you in is right!" Meg said. "You know you're not you. You know you've never in your life called me *dear sister.*"

"Shut up a minute, Meg," Calvin whispered to her. He looked up at the man with red eyes. "Okay, have your henchmen let us go and stop talking to us through Charles. We know it's you talking, or whatever's talking through you. Anyhow, we know you have Charles hypnotized."

"A most primitive way of putting it," the man with red eyes murmured. He gestured slightly with one finger, and Meg and Calvin were released.

"Thanks," Calvin said wryly. "Now, if you are our friend, will you tell us who—or what—you are?"

"It is not necessary for you to know who I am. I am the Prime Coordinator, that is all you need to know."

"But you're being spoken through, aren't you, just like Charles Wallace? Are you hypnotized, too?"

"I told you that was too primitive a word, without the correct connotations."

"Is it you who are going to take us to Mr. Murry?"

"No. It is not necessary, nor is it possible, for me to leave here. Charles Wallace will conduct you."

"Charles Wallace?"

"Yes."

"When?"

"Now." The man with red eyes made the frightening grimace that passed for his smile. "Yes, I think it might as well be now."

Charles Wallace gave a slight jerk of his head, saying, "Come," and started to walk in a strange, gliding, mechanical manner. Calvin followed him. Meg hesitated, looking from the man with red eyes to Charles and Calvin. She wanted to reach out and grab Calvin's hand, but it seemed that ever since they had begun their journeyings she had been looking for a hand to hold, so she stuffed her fists into her pockets and walked along behind the two boys. — I've got to be brave, she said to herself. —I *will* be.

They moved down a long, white, and seemingly endless corridor. Charles Wallace continued the jerky rhythm of his walk and did not once look back to see if they were with him.

Suddenly Meg broke into a run and caught up with Calvin. "Cal," she said, "listen. Quick. Remember Mrs. Whatsit said your gift was communication and that was what she was giving you. We've been trying to fight Charles physically, and that isn't any good. Can't you try to communicate with him? Can't you try to get in to him?"

"Golly day, you're right." Calvin's face lit up with hope, and his eyes, which had been somber, regained their usual sparkle. "I've been in such a swivet— It may not do any good, but at least I can try." They quickened their pace until they were level with Charles Wallace. Calvin reached out for his arm, but Charles flung it off.

"Leave me alone," he snarled.

"I'm not going to hurt you, old sport," Calvin said. "I'm just trying to be friendly. Let's make it up, hunh?"

"You mean you're coming around?" Charles Wallace asked.

"Sure," Calvin's voice was coaxing. "We're reasonable people, after all. Just look at me for a minute, Charlibus."

Charles Wallace stopped and turned slowly to look at Calvin with his cold, vacant eyes. Calvin looked back, and Meg could feel the intensity of his concentration. An enormous shudder shook Charles Wallace. For a brief flash his eyes seemed to see. Then his whole body twirled wildly, and went rigid. He started his marionette's walk again. "I should have known better," he said. "If you want to see Murry you'd better come with me and not try any more hanky-panky."

"Is that what you call your father—Murry?" Calvin asked. Meg could see that he was angry and upset at his near success.

"Father? What is a father?" Charles Wallace intoned. "Merely another misconception. If you feel the need of a father, then I would suggest that you turn to IT."

IT again.

"Who's this IT?" Meg asked.

"All in good time," Charles Wallace said. "You're not ready for IT yet. First of all I will tell you something about this beautiful, enlightened planet of Camazotz." His voice took on the dry, pedantic tones of Mr. Jenkins. "Perhaps you do not realize that on Camazotz we have conquered all illness, all deformity—"

"We?" Calvin interrupted.

Charles continued as though he had not heard. And of course he hadn't, Meg thought. "We let no one suffer. It is so much kinder simply to annihilate anyone who is ill. Nobody has weeks and weeks of runny noses and sore throats. Rather than endure such discomfort they are simply put to sleep."

"You mean they're put to sleep while they have a cold, or that they're murdered?" Calvin demanded.

"Murder is a most primitive word," Charles Wallace said. "There is no such thing as murder on Camazotz. IT takes care of all such things." He moved jerkily to the wall of the corridor, stood still for a moment, then raised his hand. The wall flickered, quivered, grew transparent. Charles Wallace walked through it, beckoned to Meg and Calvin, and they followed. They were in a small, square room from which radiated a dull, sulphurous light. There was something ominous to Meg in the very compactness of the room, as though the walls, the ceiling, the floor might move together and crush anybody rash enough to enter.

"How did you do that?" Calvin asked Charles.

"Do what?"

"Make the wall—open—like that."

"I merely rearranged the atoms," Charles Wallace said loftily. "You've studied atoms in school, haven't you?"

"Sure, but—"

"Then you know enough to know that matter isn't solid, don't you? That you, Calvin, consist mostly of empty space? That if all the matter in you came together you'd be the size of the head of a pin? That's plain scientific fact, isn't it?"

"Yes, but—"

"So I simply pushed the atoms aside and we walked through the space between them." Meg's stomach seemed to drop, and she realized that the square box in which they stood must be an elevator and that they had started to move upward with great speed. The yellow light lit up their faces, and the pale blue of Charles's eyes absorbed the yellow and turned green.

Calvin licked his lips. "Where are we going?"

"Up." Charles continued his lecture. "On Camazotz we are all happy because we are all alike. Differences create problems. You know that, don't you, dear sister?"

"No," Meg said.

"Oh, yes, you do. You've seen at home how true it is. You know that's the reason you're not happy at school. Because you're different."

"*I'm* different, and I'm happy," Calvin said.

"But you pretend that you *aren't* different."

"I'm different, and I like being different." Calvin's voice was unnaturally loud.

"Maybe I don't like being different," Meg said, "but I don't want to be like everybody else, either."

Charles Wallace raised his hand and the motion of the square box ceased and one of the walls seemed to disappear. Charles stepped out, Meg and Calvin following him, Calvin just barely making it before the wall came into being again, and they could no longer see where the opening had been.

"You wanted Calvin to get left behind, didn't you?" Meg said.

"I am merely trying to teach you to stay on your toes. I warn you, if I have any more trouble from either of you, I shall have to take you to IT."

As the word IT fell from Charles's lips, again Meg felt as though she had been touched by something slimy and horrible. "So what is this IT?" she asked.

"You might call IT the Boss." Then Charles Wallace giggled, a giggle that was the most sinister sound Meg had ever heard. "IT sometimes calls ITself the Happiest Sadist."

Meg spoke coldly, to cover her fear. "I don't know what you're talking about."

"That's s-a-d-i-s-t, not s-a-d-d-e-s-t, you know," Charles Wallace said, and giggled again. "Lots of people don't pronounce it correctly."

"Well, I don't care," Meg said defiantly. "I don't ever want to see IT, and that's that."

Charles Wallace's strange, monotonous voice ground against her ears. "Meg, you're supposed to have *some* mind. Why do you think we have wars at home? Why do you think people get confused and unhappy? Because they all live their own, separate, individual lives. I've been trying to explain to you in the simplest possible way that on Camazotz individuals have been done away with. Camazotz is ONE mind. It's IT. And that's why everybody's so happy and efficient. That's what old witches like Mrs. Whatsit don't want to have happen at home."

"She's not a witch," Meg interrupted.

"No?"

"No," Calvin said. "You know she's not. You know that's just their game. Their way, maybe, of laughing in the dark."

"In the dark is correct," Charles continued. "They want us to go on being confused instead of properly organized."

Meg shook her head violently. "No!" she shouted. "I know our world isn't perfect, Charles, but it's better than this. This isn't the only alternative! It can't be!"

"Nobody suffers here," Charles intoned. "Nobody is ever unhappy."

"But nobody's ever happy, either," Meg said earnestly. "Maybe if you aren't unhappy sometimes you don't know how to be happy. Calvin, I want to go home."

"We can't leave Charles," Calvin told her, "and we can't go before we've found your father. You know that. But you're right, Meg, and Mrs. Which is right. This is Evil."

Charles Wallace shook his head, and scorn and disapproval seemed to emanate from him. "Come. We're wasting time." He moved rapidly down the corridor, but continued to speak. "How dreadful it is to be low, individual organisms. Tch-tch-tch." His pace quickened from step to step, his short legs flashing, so that Meg and Calvin almost had to run to keep up with him. "Now see this," he said. He raised his hand and suddenly they could see through one of the walls into a small room. In the room a little boy was bouncing a ball. He was bouncing it in rhythm, and the walls of his little cell seemed to pulse with the rhythm of the ball. And each time the ball bounced he screamed as though he were in pain.

"That's the little boy we saw this afternoon," Calvin said sharply, "the little boy who wasn't bouncing the ball like the others."

Charles Wallace giggled again. "Yes. Every once in a while there's a little trouble with cooperation, but it's easily taken care of. After today he'll never desire to deviate again. Ah, here we are."

He moved rapidly down the corridor and again held up his hand to make the wall transparent. They looked into another small room or cell. In the center of it was a large, round, transparent column, and inside this column was a man.

"FATHER!" Meg screamed.

Chapter 9

IT

Meg rushed at the man imprisoned in the column, but as she reached what seemed to be the open door she was hurled back as though she had crashed into a brick wall.

Calvin caught her. "It's just transparent like glass this time," he told her. "We can't go through it."

Meg was so sick and dizzy from the impact that she could not answer. For a moment she was afraid that she would throw up or faint. Charles Wallace laughed again, the laugh that was not his own, and it was this that saved her, for once more anger overcame her pain and fear. Charles Wallace, her own real, dear Charles Wallace, never laughed at her when she hurt herself. Instead, his arms would go quickly around her neck and he would press his soft cheek against hers in loving comfort. But the demon Charles Wallace snickered. She turned away from him and looked again at the man in the column.

"Oh, Father—" she whispered longingly, but the man in the column did not move to look at her. The horn-rimmed glasses, which always seemed so much a part of him, were gone, and the expression of his eyes was turned inward, as though he were deep in thought. He had grown a beard, and the silky brown was shot with gray. His hair, too, had not been cut. It wasn't just the overlong hair of the man in the snapshot at Cape Canaveral; it was pushed back from his high forehead and fell softly almost to his shoulders, so that he looked like someone in another century, or a shipwrecked sailor. But there was no question, despite the change in him, that he was her father, her own beloved father.

"My, he looks a mess, doesn't he?" Charles Wallace said, and sniggered.

Meg swung on him with sick rage. "Charles, that's Father! Father!"

"So what?"

Meg turned away from him and held out her arms to the man in the column.

"He doesn't see us, Meg," Calvin said gently.

"Why? Why?"

"I think it's sort of like those little peepholes they have in apartments, in the front doors," Calvin explained. "You know. From inside you can look through and see everything. And from outside you can't see anything at all. We can see him, but he can't see us."

"Charles!" Meg pleaded. "Let me in to Father!"

"Why?" Charles asked placidly.

Meg remembered that when they were in the room with the man with red eyes she had knocked Charles Wallace back into himself when she tackled him and his head cracked the floor; so she hurled herself at him. But before she could reach him his fist shot out and punched her hard in the stomach. She gasped for breath. Sickly, she turned away from her brother, back to the transparent wall. There was the cell, there was the column with her father inside. Although she could see him, although she was almost close enough to touch him, he seemed farther away than he had been when she had pointed him out to Calvin in the picture on the piano. He stood there quietly as though frozen in a column of ice, an expression of suffering and endurance on his face that pierced into her heart like an arrow.

"You say you want to help Father?" Charles Wallace's voice came from behind her, with no emotion whatsoever.

"Yes. Don't you?" Meg demanded, swinging around and glaring at him.

"But of course. That is why we are here."

"Then what do we *do?*" Meg tried to keep the franticness out of her voice, trying to sound as drained of feeling as Charles, but nevertheless ending on a squeak.

"You must do as I have done, and go in to IT," Charles said.

"No."

"I can see you don't really want to save Father."

"How will my being a zombie save Father?"

"You will just have to take my word for it, Margaret," came the cold, flat voice from Charles Wallace. "IT wants you and IT will get you. Don't forget that I, too, am part of IT, now. You know I wouldn't have done IT if IT weren't the right thing to do."

"Calvin," Meg asked in agony, "will it really save Father?"

But Calvin was paying no attention to her. He seemed to be concentrating with all his power on Charles Wallace. He stared into the pale blue that was all that was left of Charles Wallace's eyes. *"And, for thou wast a spirit too delicate/To act her earthy and abhorr'd commands . . . /she did confine thee . . . into a cloven pine—*" he whispered, and Meg recognized Mrs. Who's words to him.

For a moment Charles Wallace seemed to listen. Then he shrugged and turned away. Calvin followed him, trying to keep his eyes focused on Charles's. "If you want a witch, Charles," he said, "IT's the witch. Not our ladies. Good thing I had *The Tempest* at school this year, isn't it, Charles? It was the witch who put Ariel in the cloven pine, wasn't it?"

Charles Wallace's voice seemed to come from a great distance. "Stop staring at me."

Breathing quickly with excitement, Calvin continued to pin Charles Wallace with his stare. "You're like Ariel in the cloven pine, Charles. And I can let you out. Look at me, Charles. Come back to us."

Again the shudder went through Charles Wallace.

Calvin's intense voice hit at him. "Come back, Charles. Come back to us."

Again Charles shuddered. And then it was as though an invisible hand had smacked against his chest and knocked him to the ground, and the stare with which Calvin had held him was broken. Charles sat there on the floor of the corridor whimpering, not a small boy's sound, but a fearful, animal noise.

"Calvin." Meg turned on him, clasping her hands intensely. "Try to get to Father."

Calvin shook his head. "Charles almost came out. I almost did it. He almost came back to us."

"Try Father," Meg said again.

"How?"

"Your cloven pine thing. Isn't Father imprisoned in a cloven pine even more than Charles? Look at him, in that column there. Get him out, Calvin."

Calvin spoke in an exhausted way. "Meg. I don't

know what to do. I don't know how to get in. Meg, they're asking too much of us."

"Mrs. Who's spectacles!" Meg said suddenly. Mrs. Who had told her to use them only as a last resort, and surely that was now. She reached into her pocket and the spectacles were there, cool and light and comforting. With trembling fingers she pulled them out.

"Give me those spectacles!" Charles Wallace's voice came in a harsh command, and he scrambled up off the floor and ran at her.

She barely had time to snatch off her own glasses and put on Mrs. Who's, and, as it was, one earpiece dropped down her cheek and they barely stayed on her nose. As Charles Wallace lunged at her she flung herself against the transparent door and she was through it. She was in the cell with the imprisoning column that held her father. With trembling fingers she straightened Mrs. Who's glasses and put her own in her pocket.

"Give them to me," came Charles Wallace's menacing voice, and he was in the cell with her, with Calvin on the outside pounding frantically to get in.

Meg kicked at Charles Wallace and ran at the column. She felt as though she were going through something dark and cold. But she was through. "Father!" she cried. And she was in his arms.

This was the moment for which she had been waiting, not only since Mrs. Which whisked them off on their journeys, but during the long months and years before, when the letters had stopped coming, when people made remarks about Charles Wallace, when Mrs. Murry showed a rare flash of loneliness or grief. This was the moment that meant that now and forever everything would be all right.

As she pressed against her father all was forgotten

except joy. There was only the peace and comfort of leaning against him, the wonder of the protecting circle of his arms, the feeling of complete reassurance and safety that his presence always gave her.

Her voice broke on a happy sob. "Oh, Father! Oh, Father!"

"Meg!" he cried in glad surprise. "Meg, what are you doing here? Where's your mother? Where are the boys?"

She looked out of the column, and there was Charles Wallace in the cell, an alien expression distorting his face. She turned back to her father. There was no more time for greeting, for joy, for explanations. "We have to go to Charles Wallace," she said, her words tense. "Quickly."

Her father's hands were moving gropingly over her face, and as she felt the touch of his strong, gentle fingers, she realized with a flooding of horror that she could see him, that she could see Charles in the cell and Calvin in the corridor, but her father could not see them, could not see her. She looked at him in panic, but his eyes were the same steady blue that she remembered. She moved her hand brusquely across his line of vision, but he did not blink.

"Father!" she cried. "Father! Can't you see me?"

His arms went around her again in a comforting, reassuring gesture. "No, Meg."

"But, Father, I can see you—" Her voice trailed off. Suddenly she shoved Mrs. Who's glasses down her nose and peered over them, and immediately she was in complete and utter darkness. She snatched them off her face and thrust them at her father. "Here."

His fingers closed about the spectacles. "Darling," he said, "I'm afraid your glasses won't help."

"But they're Mrs. Who's, they aren't mine," she

explained, not realizing that her words would sound like gibberish to him. "Please try them, Father. Please!" She waited while she felt him fumbling in the dark. "Can you see now?" she asked. "Can you see now, Father?"

"Yes," he said. "Yes. The wall is transparent, now. How extraordinary! I could almost see the atoms rearranging!" His voice had its old, familiar sound of excitement and discovery. It was the way he sounded sometimes when he came home from his laboratory after a good day and began to tell his wife about his work. Then he cried out, "Charles! Charles Wallace!" And then, "Meg, what's happened to him? What's wrong? That *is* Charles, isn't it?"

"IT has him, Father," she explained tensely. "He's gone into IT. Father, we have to help him."

For a long moment Mr. Murry was silent. The silence was filled with the words he was thinking and would not speak out loud to his daughter. Then he said, "Meg, I'm in prison here. I have been for—"

"Father, these walls. You can go through them. I came through the column to get in to you. It was Mrs. Who's glasses."

Mr. Murry did not stop to ask who Mrs. Who was. He slapped his hand against the translucent column. "It seems solid enough."

"But I got in," Meg repeated. "I'm here. Maybe the glasses help the atoms rearrange. Try it, Father."

She waited, breathlessly, and after a moment she realized that she was alone in the column. She put out her hands in the darkness and felt its smooth surface curving about her on all sides. She seemed utterly alone, the silence and darkness impenetrable forever. She fought down panic until she heard her father's voice coming to her very faintly.

"I'm coming back in for you, Meg."

It was almost a tangible feeling as the atoms of the strange material seemed to part to let him through to her. In their beach house at Cape Canaveral there had been a curtain between dining and living room made of long strands of rice. It looked like a solid curtain, but you could walk right through it. At first Meg had flinched each time she came up to the curtain; but gradually she got used to it and would go running right through, leaving the long strands of rice swinging behind her. Perhaps the atoms of these walls were arranged in somewhat the same fashion.

"Put your arms around my neck, Meg," Mr. Murry said. "Hold on to me tightly. Close your eyes and don't be afraid." He picked her up and she wrapped her long legs around his waist and clung to his neck. With Mrs. Who's spectacles on she had felt only a faint darkness and coldness as she moved through the column. Without the glasses she felt the same awful clamminess she had felt when they tessered through the outer darkness of Camazotz. Whatever the Black Thing was to which Camazotz had submitted, it was within as well as without the planet. For a moment it seemed that the chill darkness would tear her from her father's arms. She tried to scream, but within that icy horror no sound was possible. Her father's arms tightened about her, and she clung to his neck in a strangle hold, but she was no longer lost in panic. She knew that if her father could not get her through the wall he would stay with her rather than leave her; she knew that she was safe as long as she was in his arms.

Then they were outside. The column rose up in the middle of the room, crystal clear and empty.

Meg blinked at the blurred figures of Charles and her father, and wondered why they did not clear. Then she grabbed her own glasses out of her pocket and put them on, and her myopic eyes were able to focus.

Charles Wallace was tapping one foot impatiently against the floor. "IT is not pleased," he said. "IT is not pleased at all."

Mr. Murry released Meg and knelt in front of the little boy. "Charles," his voice was tender. "Charles Wallace."

"What do you want?"

"I'm your father, Charles. Look at me."

The pale blue eyes seemed to focus on Mr. Murry's face. "Hi, Pop," came an insolent voice.

"That isn't Charles!" Meg cried. "Oh, Father, Charles isn't like that. IT has him."

"Yes." Mr. Murry sounded tired. "I see." He held his arms out. "Charles. Come here."

Father will make it all right, Meg thought. Everything will be all right now.

Charles did not move toward the outstretched arms. He stood a few feet away from his father, and he did not look at him.

"Look at me," Mr. Murry commanded.

"No."

Mr. Murry's voice became harsh. "When you speak to me you will say 'No, Father,' or 'No, sir.'"

"Come off it, Pop," came the cold voice from Charles Wallace—Charles Wallace who, outside Camazotz, had been strange, had been different, but never rude. "You're not the boss around here."

Meg could see Calvin pounding again on the glass wall. "Calvin!" she called.

"He can't hear you," Charles said. He made a horrible face at Calvin, and then he thumbed his nose.

"Who's Calvin?" Mr. Murry asked.

"He's—" Meg started, but Charles Wallace cut her short.

"You'll have to defer your explanations. Let's go."

"Go where?"

"To IT."

"No," Mr. Murry said. "You can't take Meg there."

"Oh, can't I!"

"No, you cannot. You're my son, Charles, and I'm afraid you will have to do as I say."

"But he *isn't* Charles!" Meg cried in anguish. Why didn't her father understand? "Charles is nothing like that, Father! You know he's nothing like that!"

"He was only a baby when I left," Mr. Murry said heavily.

"Father, it's IT talking through Charles. IT isn't Charles. He's—he's bewitched."

"Fairy tales again," Charles said.

"You know IT, Father?" Meg asked.

"Yes."

"Have you seen IT?"

"Yes, Meg." Again his voice sounded exhausted. "Yes. I have." He turned to Charles. "You know she wouldn't be able to hold out."

"Exactly," Charles said.

"Father, you can't talk to him as though he were Charles! Ask Calvin! Calvin will tell you."

"Come along," Charles Wallace said. "We must go." He held up his hand carelessly and walked out of the cell, and there was nothing for Meg and Mr. Murry to do but to follow.

As they stepped into the corridor Meg caught at her father's sleeve. "Calvin, here's Father!"

Calvin turned anxiously toward them. His freckles and his hair stood out brilliantly against his white face.

"Make your introductions later," Charles Wallace said. "IT does not like to be kept waiting." He walked down the corridor, his gait seeming to get more jerky with each step. The others followed, walking rapidly to keep up.

"Does your father know about the Mrs. W's?" Calvin asked Meg.

"There hasn't been time for anything. Everything's awful." Despair settled like a stone in the pit of Meg's stomach. She had been so certain that the moment she found her father everything would be all right. Everything would be settled. All the problems would be taken out of her hands. She would no longer be responsible for anything.

And instead of this happy and expected outcome, they seemed to be encountering all kinds of new troubles.

"He doesn't understand about Charles," she whispered to Calvin, looking unhappily at her father's back as he walked behind the little boy.

"Where are we going?" Calvin asked.

"To IT. Calvin, I don't want to go! I can't!" She stopped, but Charles continued his jerky pace.

"We can't leave Charles," Calvin said. "They wouldn't like it."

"Who woundn't?"

"Mrs. Whatsit & Co."

"But they've betrayed us! They brought us here to this terrible place and abandoned us!"

Calvin looked at her in surprise. "You sit down and give up if you like," he said. "I'm sticking with Charles." He ran to keep up with Charles Wallace and Mr. Murry.

"I didn't mean—" Meg started, and pounded after them.

Just as she caught up with them Charles Wallace stopped and raised his hand, and there was the elevator again, its yellow light sinister. Meg felt her stomach jerk as the swift descent began. They were silent until the motion stopped, silent as they followed Charles Wallace through long corridors and out into the street. The CENTRAL Central Intelligence Building loomed up, stark and angular, behind them.

—Do something, Meg implored her father silently. —Do something. Help. Save us.

They turned a corner, and at the end of the street was a strange, domelike building. Its walls glowed with a flicker of violet flame. Its silvery roof pulsed with ominous light. The light was neither warm nor cold, but it seemed to reach out and touch them. This, Meg was sure, must be where IT was waiting for them.

They moved down the street, more slowly now, and as they came closer to the domed building the violet flickering seemed to reach out, to envelop them, to suck them in: they were inside.

Meg could feel a rhythmical pulsing. It was a pulsing not only about her, but in her as well, as though the rhythm of her heart and lungs was no longer her own but was being worked by some outside force. The closest she had come to the feeling before was when she had been practicing artificial respiration with Girl Scouts, and the leader, an immensely powerful woman, had been working on Meg, intoning OUT goes the bad air, IN comes the good! while her heavy hands pressed, released, pressed, released.

Meg gasped, trying to breathe at her own normal rate, but the inexorable beat within and without continued. For a moment she could neither move nor look around to see what was happening to the others. She simply had to stand there, trying to balance herself into the artificial rhythm of her heart and lungs. Her eyes seemed to swim in a sea of red.

Then things began to clear, and she could breathe without gasping like a beached fish, and she could look about the great, circular, domed building. It was completely empty except for the pulse, which seemed a tangible thing, and a round dais exactly in the center. On the dais lay—what? Meg could not tell, and yet she knew that it was from this that the rhythm came. She stepped forward tentatively. She felt that she was beyond fear now. Charles Wallace was no longer Charles Wallace. Her father had been found but he had not made everything all right. Instead everything was worse than ever, and her adored father was bearded and thin and white and not omnipotent after all. No matter what happened next, things could be no more terrible or frightening than they already were.

Oh, couldn't they?

As she continued to step slowly forward, at last she realized what the Thing on the dais was.

IT was a brain.

A disembodied brain. An oversized brain, just enough larger than normal to be completely revolting and terrifying. A living brain. A brain that pulsed and quivered, that seized and commanded. No wonder the brain was called IT. IT was the most horrible, the most repellent thing she had ever seen, far more nauseating than anything she had ever imagined with her conscious mind, or that had ever tormented her in her most terrible nightmares.

But as she had felt she was beyond fear, so now she was beyond screaming.

She looked at Charles Wallace, and he stood there, turned towards IT, his jaw hanging slightly loose; and his vacant blue eyes slowly twirled.

Oh, yes, things could always be worse. These twirling eyes within Charles Wallace's soft round face made Meg icy cold inside and out.

She looked away from Charles Wallace and at her father. Her father stood there with Mrs. Who's glasses still perched on his nose—did he remember that he had them on?—and he shouted to Calvin. "Don't give in!"

"I won't! Help Meg!" Calvin yelled back. It was absolutely silent within the dome, and yet Meg realized that the only way to speak was to shout with all the power possible. For everywhere she looked, everywhere she turned, was the rhythm, and as it continued to control the systole and diastole of her heart, the intake and outlet of her breath, the red miasma began to creep before her eyes again, and she was afraid that she was going to lose consciousness, and if she did that she would be completely in the power of IT.

Mrs. Whatsit had said, "Meg, I give you your faults."

What were her greatest faults? Anger, impatience, stubbornness. Yes, it was to her faults that she turned to save herself now.

With an immense effort she tried to breathe against the rhythm of IT. But IT's power was too strong. Each time she managed to take a breath out of rhythm an iron hand seemed to squeeze her heart and lungs.

Then she remembered that when they had been standing before the man with red eyes, and the man with red eyes had been intoning the multiplication table at them, Charles Wallace had fought against his power by shouting out nursery rhymes, and Calvin by the Gettysburg Address.

"*Georgie, porgie, pudding and pie,*" she yelled. "*Kissed the girls and made them cry.*"

That was no good. It was too easy for nursery rhymes to fall into the rhythm of IT.

She didn't know the Gettysburg Address. How did the Declaration of Independence begin? She had memorized it only that winter, not because she was required to at school, but simply because she liked it.

"We hold these truths to be self-evident!" she shouted, "that all men are created equal, that they are endowed by their creator with certain unalienable rights, that among these are life, liberty, and the pursuit of happiness."

As she cried out the words she felt a mind moving in on her own, felt IT seizing, squeezing her brain. Then she realized that Charles Wallace was speaking, or being spoken through by IT.

"But that's exactly what we have on Camazotz. Complete equality. Everybody exactly alike."

For a moment her brain reeled with confusion. Then came a moment of blazing truth. "No!" she cried triumphantly. "*Like* and *equal* are not the same thing at all!"

"Good girl, Meg!" her father shouted at her.

But Charles Wallace continued as though there had been no interruption. "In Camazotz all are equal. In Camazotz everybody is the same as everybody else," but he gave her no argument, provided no answer, and she held on to her moment of revelation.

Like and equal are two entirely different things.

For the moment she had escaped from the power of IT.

But how?

She knew that her own puny little brain was no match for this great, bodiless, pulsing, writhing mass on the round dais. She shuddered as she looked at IT. In the lab at school there was a human brain preserved in formaldehyde, and the seniors preparing for college had to take it out and look at it and study it. Meg had felt that when that day came she would never be able to endure it. But now she thought that if only she had a dissecting knife she would slash at IT, cutting ruthlessly through cerebrum, cerebellum.

Words spoke within her, directly this time, not through Charles. "Don't you realize that if you destroy me, you also destroy your little brother?"

If that great brain were cut, were crushed, would every mind under IT's control on Camazotz die, too? Charles Wallace and the man with red eyes and the man who ran the number-one spelling machine on the second-grade level and all the children playing ball and skipping rope and all the mothers and all the men and women going in and out of the buildings? Was their life completely dependent on IT? Were they beyond all possibility of salvation?

She felt the brain reaching at her again as she let her stubborn control slip. Red fog glazed her eyes.

Faintly she heard her father's voice, though she knew he was shouting at the top of his lungs. "The periodic table of elements, Meg! Say it!"

A picture flashed into her mind of winter evenings spent sitting before the open fire and studying with her father. "Hydrogen. Helium," she started obediently. Keep them in their proper atomic order. What next. She knew it. Yes. "Lithium. Beryllium. Boron. Carbon. Nitrogen. Oxygen. Fluorine." She shouted the words at her father, turned away from IT. "Neon. Sodium. Magnesium. Aluminum. Silicon. Phosphorus."

"Too rhythmical," her father shouted. "What's the square root of five?"

For a moment she was able to concentrate. Rack your brains yourself, Meg. Don't let IT rack them. "The square root of five is 2.236," she cried triumphantly, "because 2.236 times 2.236 equals 5!"

"What's the square root of seven?"

"The square root of seven is—" She broke off. She wasn't holding out. IT was getting at her, and she couldn't concentrate, not even on math, and soon she, too, would be absorbed in IT, she would *be* an IT.

"Tesser, sir!" she heard Calvin's voice through the red darkness. "Tesser!"

She felt her father grab her by the wrist, there was a terrible jerk that seemed to break every bone in her body, then the dark nothing of tessering.

If tessering with Mrs. Whatsit, Mrs. Who, and Mrs. Which had been a strange and fearful experience, it was nothing like tessering with her father. After all, Mrs. Which was experienced at it, and Mr. Murry—how did he know anything about it at all? Meg felt that she was being torn apart by a whirlwind. She was lost in an agony of pain that finally dissolved into the darkness of complete unconsciousness.

Chapter 10

ABSOLUTE ZERO

The first sign of returning consciousness was cold. Then sound. She was aware of voices that seemed to be traveling through her across an arctic waste. Slowly the icy sounds cleared and she realized that the voices belonged to her father and Calvin. She did not hear Charles Wallace. She tried to open her eyes but the lids would not move. She tried to sit up, but she could not stir. She struggled to turn over, to move her hands, her feet, but nothing happened. She knew that she had a body, but it was as lifeless as marble.

She heard Calvin's frozen voice: "Her heart is beating so slowly—"

Her father's voice: "But it's beating. She's alive."

"Barely."

"We couldn't find a heartbeat at all at first. We thought she was dead."

"Yes."

"And then we could feel her heart, very faintly, the beats very far apart. And then it got stronger. So all we have to do is wait." Her father's words sounded brittle in her ears, as though they were being chipped out of ice.

Calvin: "Yes. You're right, sir."

She wanted to call out to them. "I'm alive! I'm very much alive! Only I've been turned to stone."

But she could not call out any more than she could move.

Calvin's voice again. "Anyhow you got her away from IT. You got us both away and we couldn't have gone on holding out. IT's so much more powerful and strong than—How *did* we stay out, sir? How did we manage as long as we did?"

Her father: "Because IT's completely unused to being refused. That's the only reason I could keep from being absorbed, too. No mind has tried to hold out against IT for so many thousands of centuries that certain centers have become soft and atrophied through lack of use. If you hadn't come to me when you did I'm not sure how much longer I would have lasted. I was on the point of giving in."

Calvin: "Oh, no, sir—"

Her father: "Yes. Nothing seemed important any more but rest, and of course IT offered me complete rest. I had almost come to the conclusion that I was wrong to fight, that IT was right after all, and everything I believed in most passionately was nothing but a madman's dream. But then you and Meg came in to me, broke through my prison, and hope and faith returned."

Calvin: "Sir, why were you on Camazotz at all? Was there a particular reason for going there?"

Her father, with a frigid laugh: "Going to Camazotz was a complete accident. I never intended even to leave our own solar system. I was heading for Mars. Tessering is even more complicated than we had expected."

Calvin: "Sir, how was IT able to get Charles Wallace before it got Meg and me?"

Her father: "From what you've told me it's because Charles Wallace thought he could deliberately go into IT and return. He trusted too much to his own strength—listen!—I think the heartbeat is getting stronger!"

His words no longer sounded to her quite as frozen. Was it his words that were ice, or her ears? Why did she hear only her father and Calvin? Why didn't Charles Wallace speak?

Silence. A long silence. Then Calvin's voice again: "Can't we do anything? Can't we look for help? Do we just have to go on waiting?"

Her father: "We can't leave her. And we must stay together. We must *not* be afraid to take time."

Calvin: "You mean we were? We rushed into things on Camazotz too fast, and Charles Wallace rushed in too fast, and that's why he got caught?"

"Maybe. I'm not sure. I don't know enough yet. Time is different on Camazotz, anyhow. Our time, inadequate though it is, at least is straightforward. It may not be even fully one-dimensional, because it can't move back and forth on its line, only ahead; but at least it's consistent in its direction. Time on Camazotz seems to be inverted, turned in on itself. So I have no idea whether I was imprisoned in that column for centuries or only for minutes." Silence for a moment. Then her father's voice again. "I think I feel a pulse in her wrist now."

Meg could not feel his fingers against her wrist. She could not feel her wrist at all. Her body was still stone, but her mind was beginning to be capable of movement. She tried desperately to make some kind of a sound, a signal to them, but nothing happened.

Their voices started again. Calvin: "About your project, sir. Were you on it alone?"

Her father: "Oh, no. There were half a dozen of us working on it and I daresay a number of others we don't know about. Certainly we weren't the only nation to investigate along that line. It's not really a new idea. But we did try very hard not to let it be known abroad that we were trying to make it practicable."

"Did you come to Camazotz alone? Or were there others with you?"

"I came alone. You see, Calvin, there was no way to try it out ahead with rats or monkeys or dogs. And we had no idea whether it would really work or whether it would be complete bodily disintegration. Playing with time and space is a dangerous game."

"But why you, sir?"

"I wasn't the first. We drew straws, and I was second."

"What happened to the first man?"

"We don't—look! Did her eyelids move?" Silence. Then: "No. It was only a shadow."

But I *did* blink, Meg tried to tell them. I'm sure I did. And I can hear you! *Do* something!

But there was only another long silence, during which perhaps they were looking at her, watching for another shadow, another flicker. Then she heard her father's voice again, quiet, a little warmer, more like his own voice. "We drew straws, and I was second. We know Hank went. We saw him go. We saw him vanish right in front of the rest of us. He was there and then he wasn't. We were to wait for a year for his return or for some message. We waited. Nothing."

Calvin, his voice cracking: "Jeepers, sir. You must have been in sort of a flap."

Her father: "Yes. It's a frightening as well as an exciting thing to discover that matter and energy *are* the same thing, that size is an illusion, and that time is a material substance. We can know this, but it's far more than we can understand with our puny little brains. I think you will be able to comprehend far more than I. And Charles Wallace even more than you."

"Yes, but what happened, please, sir, after the first man?"

Meg could hear her father sigh. "Then it was my turn. I went. And here I am. A wiser and a humbler man. I'm sure I haven't been gone two years. Now that you've come I have some hope that I may be able to return in time. One thing I have to tell the others is that we know nothing."

Calvin: "What do you mean, sir?"

Her father: "Just what I say. We're children playing with dynamite. In our mad rush we've plunged into this before—"

With a desperate effort Meg made a sound. It wasn't a very loud sound, but it was a sound. Mr. Murry stopped. "Hush. Listen."

Meg made a strange, croaking noise. She found that she could pull open her eyelids. They felt heavier than marble but she managed to raise them. Her father and Calvin were hovering over her. She did not see Charles Wallace. Where was he?

She was lying in an open field of what looked like rusty, stubby grass. She blinked, slowly, and with difficulty.

"Meg," her father said. "Meg. Are you all right?"

Her tongue felt like a stone tongue in her mouth, but she managed to croak, "I can't move."

"Try," Calvin urged. He sounded now as though he were very angry with her. "Wiggle your toes. Wiggle your fingers."

"I can't. Where's Charles Wallace?" Her words

were blunted by the stone tongue. Perhaps they could not understand her, for there was no answer.

"We were knocked out for a minute, too," Calvin was saying. "You'll be all right, Meg. Don't get panicky." He was crouched over her, and though his voice continued to sound cross he was peering at her with anxious eyes. She knew that she must still have her glasses on because she could see him clearly, his freckles, his stubby black lashes, the bright blue of his eyes.

Her father was kneeling on her other side. The round lenses of Mrs. Who's glasses still blurred his eyes. He took one of her hands and rubbed it between his. "Can you feel my fingers?" He sounded quite calm, as though there were nothing extra-ordinary in having her completely paralyzed. At the quiet of his voice she felt calmer. Then she saw that there were great drops of sweat standing out on his forehead, and she noticed vaguely that the gentle breeze that touched her cheeks was cool. At first his words had been frozen and now the wind was mild: was it icy cold here or warm? "Can you feel my fingers?" he asked again.

Yes, now she could feel a pressure against her wrist, but she could not nod. "Where's Charles Wallace?" Her words were a little less blurred. Her tongue, her lips were beginning to feel cold and numb, as though she had been given a massive dose of novacaine at the dentist's. She realized with a start that her body and limbs were cold, that not only was she not warm, she was frozen from head to toe, and it was this that had made her father's words seem like ice, that had paralyzed her.

"I'm frozen—" she said faintly. Camazotz hadn't been this cold, a cold that cut deeper than the wind on the bitterest of winter days at home. She was away from IT, but this unexplained iciness was almost as bad. Her father had not saved her.

Now she was able to look around a little, and everything she could see was rusty and gray. There were trees edging the field in which she lay, and their leaves were the same brown as the grass. There were plants that might have been flowers, except that they were dull and gray. In contrast to the drabness of color, to the cold that numbed her, the air was filled with a delicate, springlike fragrance, almost imperceptible as it blew softly against her face. She looked at her father and Calvin. They were both in their shirt sleeves and they looked perfectly comfortable. It was she, wrapped in their clothes, who was frozen too solid even to shiver.

"Why am I so cold?" she asked. "Where's Charles Wallace?" They did not answer. "Father, where are we?"

Mr. Murry looked at her soberly. "I don't know, Meg. I don't tesser very well. I must have overshot, somehow. We're not on Camazotz. I don't know where we are. I think you're so cold because we went through the Black Thing, and I thought for a moment it was going to tear you away from me."

"Is this a dark planet?" Slowly her tongue was beginning to thaw; her words were less blurred.

"I don't think so," Mr. Murry said, "but I know so little about anything that I can't be sure."

"You shouldn't have tried to tesser, then." She had never spoken to her father in this way before. The words seemed hardly to be hers.

Calvin looked at her, shaking his head. "It was the only thing to do. At least it got us off Camazotz."

"Why did we go without Charles Wallace? Did we just leave him there?" The words that were not really hers came out cold and accusing.

"We didn't 'just leave him,'" her father said. "Remember that the human brain is a very delicate organism, and it can be easily damaged."

"See, Meg," Calvin crouched over her, tense and worried, "if your father had tried to yank Charles away when he tessered us, and if IT had kept grabbing hold of Charles, it might have been too much for him, and we'd have lost him forever. And we had to do something right then."

"Why?"

"IT was taking us. You and I were slipping, and if your father had gone on trying to help us he wouldn't have been able to hold out much longer, either."

"*You* told him to tesser," Meg charged Calvin.

"There isn't any question of blame," Mr. Murry cut in severely. "Can you move yet?"

All Meg's faults were uppermost in her now, and they were no longer helping her. "No! And you'd better take me back to Camazotz and Charles Wallace quickly. You're supposed to be able to help!" Disappointment was as dark and corrosive in her as the Black Thing. The ugly words tumbled from her cold lips even as she herself could not believe that it was her father, her beloved, longed-for father, that she was talking to in this way. If her tears had not still been frozen they would have gushed from her eyes.

She had found her father and he had not made everything all right. Everything kept getting worse and worse. If the long search for her father was ended, and he wasn't able to overcome all their difficulties, there was nothing to guarantee that it would all come out right in the end. There was nothing left to hope for. She was frozen, and Charles Wallace was being devoured by IT, and her omnipotent father was doing nothing. She teetered on the seesaw of love and hate, and the Black Thing pushed her down into hate. "You don't even know where we are!" she cried out at her father. "We'll never see Mother or the twins again! We don't know where earth is! Or even where Camazotz is! We're lost out in space! What are you going to *do*!" She did not realize that she was as much in the power of the Black Thing as Charles Wallace.

Mr. Murry bent over her, massaging her cold fingers. She could not see his face. "My daughter, I am not a Mrs. Whatsit, a Mrs. Who, or a Mrs. Which. Yes, Calvin has told me everything he could. I am a human being, and a very fallible one. But I agree with Calvin. We were sent here for something. And we know that all things work together for good to them that love God, to them who are called according to his purpose."

"The Black Thing!" Meg cried out at him. "Why did you let it almost get me?"

"You've never tessered as well as the rest of us," Calvin reminded her. "It never bothered Charles and me as much as it did you."

"He shouldn't have taken me, then," Meg said, "until he learned to do it better."

Neither her father nor Calvin spoke. Her father continued his gentle massage. Her fingers came back to life with tingling pain. "You're hurting me!"

"Then you're feeling again," her father said quietly. "I'm afraid it *is* going to hurt, Meg."

The piercing pain moved slowly up her arms, began in her toes and legs. She started to cry out against her father when Calvin exclaimed, "Look!"

Coming toward them, moving in silence across the brown grass, were three figures.

What were they?

On Uriel there had been the magnificent creatures. On Camazotz the inhabitants had at least resembled people. What were these three strange things approaching?

They were the same dull gray color as the flowers. If they hadn't walked upright they would have seemed like animals. They moved directly toward the three human beings. They had four arms and far more than five fingers to each hand, and the fingers were not fingers, but long waving tentacles. They had heads, and they had faces. But where the faces of the creatures on Uriel had seemed far more than human faces, these seemed far less. Where the features would normally be there were several indentations, and in place of ears and hair were more tentacles. They were tall, Meg realized as they came closer, far taller than any man. They had no eyes. Just soft indentations.

Meg's rigid, frozen body tried to shudder with terror, but instead of the shudder all that came was pain. She moaned.

The Things stood over them. They appeared to be looking down at them, except that they had no eyes with which to see. Mr. Murry continued to kneel by Meg, massaging her.

He's killed us, bringing us here, Meg thought. I'll never see Charles Wallace again, or Mother, or the twins. . . .

Calvin rose to his feet. He bowed to the beasts as though they could see him. He said, "How do you do, sir—ma'am—?"

"Who are you?" the tallest of the beasts said. His voice was neither hostile nor welcoming, and it came not from the mouthlike indentation in the furry face, but from the waving tentacles.

—They'll eat us, Meg thought wildly. —They're

making me hurt. My toes—my fingers—I hurt. . . .

Calvin answered the beast's question. "We're—we're from earth. I'm not sure how we got here. We've had an accident. Meg—this girl—is—is paralyzed. She can't move. She's terribly cold. We think that's why she can't move."

One of them came up to Meg and squatted down on its huge haunches beside her, and she felt utter loathing and revulsion as it reached out a tentacle to touch her face.

But with the tentacle came the same delicate fragrance that moved across her with the breeze, and she felt a soft, tingling warmth go all through her that momentarily assuaged her pain. She felt suddenly sleepy.

I must look as strange to it as it looks to me, she thought drowsily, and then realized with a shock that of course the beast couldn't see her at all. Nevertheless a reassuring sense of safety flowed through her with the warmth which continued to seep deep into her as the beast touched her. Then it picked her up, cradling her in two of its four arms.

Mr. Murry stood up quickly. "What are you doing?"

"Taking the child."

Chapter 11

AUNT BEAST

"No!" Mr. Murry said sharply. "Please put her down."

A sense of amusement seemed to emanate from the beasts. The tallest, who seemed to be the spokesman, said, "We frighten you?"

"What are you going to do with us?" Mr. Murry asked.

The beast said, "I'm sorry, we communicate better with the other one." He turned toward Calvin. "Who are you?"

"I'm Calvin O'Keefe."

"What's that?"

"I'm a boy. A—a young man."

"You, too, are afraid?"

"I'm—not sure."

"Tell me," the beast said. "What do you suppose you'd do if three of *us* suddenly arrived on your home planet."

"Shoot you, I guess," Calvin admitted.

"Then isn't that what we should do with you?"

Calvin's freckles seemed to deepen, but he

answered quietly. "I'd really rather you didn't. I mean, the earth's my home, and I'd rather be there than anywhere in the world—I mean, the universe—and I can't wait to get back, but we make some awful bloopers there."

The smallest beast, the one holding Meg, said, "And perhaps they aren't used to visitors from other planets."

"Used to it!" Calvin exclaimed. "We've never had any, as far as I know."

"Why?"

"I don't know."

The middle beast, a tremor of trepidation in his words, said, "You aren't from a dark planet, are you?"

"No." Calvin shook his head firmly, though the beast couldn't see him. "We're—we're shadowed. But we're fighting the shadow."

The beast holding Meg questioned, "You three are fighting?"

"Yes," Calvin answered. "Now that we know about it."

The tall one turned back to Mr. Murry, speaking sternly. "You. The oldest. Man. From where have you come? Now."

Mr. Murry answered steadily. "From a planet called Camazotz." There was a mutter from the three beasts. "We do not belong there," Mr. Murry said, slowly and distinctly. "We were strangers there as we are here. I was a prisoner there, and these children rescued me. My youngest son, my baby, is still there, trapped in the dark mind of IT."

Meg tried to twist around in the beast's arms to glare at her father and Calvin. Why were they being so frank? Weren't they aware of the danger? But again her anger dissolved as the gentle warmth from the tentacles flowed through her. She realized that she could move her fingers and toes with comparative freedom, and the pain was no longer so acute.

"We must take this child back with us," the beast holding her said.

Meg shouted at her father. "Don't leave me the way you left Charles!" With this burst of terror a spasm of pain wracked her body and she gasped.

"Stop fighting," the beast told her. "You make it worse. Relax."

"That's what IT said," Meg cried. "Father! Calvin! Help!"

The beast turned toward Calvin and Mr. Murry. "This child is in danger. You must trust us."

"We have no alternative," Mr. Murry said. "Can you save her?"

"I think so."

"May I stay with her?"

"No. But you will not be far away. We feel that you are hungry, tired, that you would like to bathe and rest. And this little—what is the word?" the beast cocked its tentacles at Calvin.

"Girl," Calvin said.

"This little girl needs prompt and special care. The coldness of the—what is it you call it?"

"The Black Thing?"

"The Black Thing. Yes. The Black Thing burns unless it is counteracted properly." The three beasts stood around Meg, and it seemed that they were feeling into her with their softly waving tentacles. The movement of the tentacles was as rhythmic and flowing as the dance of an undersea plant, and lying there, cradled in the four strange arms, Meg, despite herself, felt a sense of security that was deeper than anything she had known since the days when she lay in her mother's arms in the old rocking chair and was sung to sleep. With her father's help she had been able to resist IT. Now she could hold out no longer. She leaned her head against the beast's chest, and realized that the gray body was covered with the softest, most delicate fur imaginable, and the fur had the same beautiful odor as the air.

I hope I don't smell awful to it, she thought. But then she knew with a deep sense of comfort that even if she did smell awful the beasts would forgive her. As the tall figure cradled her she could feel the frigid stiffness of her body relaxing against it. This bliss could not come to her from a thing like IT. IT could only give pain, never relieve it. The beasts must be good. They had to be good. She sighed deeply, like a very small child, and suddenly she was asleep.

When she came to herself again there was in the back of her mind a memory of pain, of agonizing pain. But the pain was over now and her body was lapped in comfort. She was lying on something wonderfully soft in an enclosed chamber. It was dark. All she could see were occasional tall moving shadows which she realized were beasts walking about. She had been stripped of her clothes, and something warm and pungent was gently being rubbed into her body. She sighed and stretched and discovered that she *could* stretch. She could move again, she was no longer paralyzed, and her body was bathed in waves of warmth. Her father had not saved her; the beasts had.

"So you are awake, little one?" The words came gently to her ears. "What a funny little tadpole you are! Is the pain gone now?"

"All gone."

"Are you warm and alive again?"

"Yes, I'm fine." She struggled to sit up.

"No, lie still, small one. You must not exert yourself as yet. We will have a fur garment for you in a moment, and then we will feed you. You must not even try to feed yourself. You must be as an infant again. The Black Thing does not relinquish its victims willingly."

"Where are Father and Calvin? Have they gone back for Charles Wallace?"

"They are eating and resting," the beast said, "and we are trying to learn about each other and see what is best to help you. We feel now that you are not dangerous, and that we will be allowed to help you."

"Why is it so dark in here?" Meg asked. She tried to look around, but all she could see was shadows. Nevertheless there was a sense of openness, a feel of a gentle breeze moving lightly about, that kept the darkness from being oppressive.

Perplexity came to her from the beast. "What is this dark? What is this light? We do not understand. Your father and the boy, Calvin, have asked this, too. They say that it is night now on our planet, and that they cannot see. They have told us that our atmosphere is what they call opaque, so that the stars are not visible, and then they were surprised that we know stars, that we know their music and the movements of their dance far better than beings like you who spend hours studying them through what you call telescopes. We do not understand what this means, *to see.*"

"Well, it's what things look like," Meg said helplessly.

"We do not know what things *look* like, as you say," the beast said. "We know what things *are* like. It must be a very limiting thing, this seeing."

"Oh, no!" Meg cried. "It's—it's the most wonderful thing in the world!"

"What a very strange world yours must be!" the beast said, "that such a peculiar-seeming thing should be of such importance. Try to tell me, what is this thing called *light* that you are able to do so little without?"

"Well, we can't see without it," Meg said, realizing that she was completely unable to explain vision and light and dark. How can you explain sight on a world where no one has ever seen and where there is no need of eyes? "Well, on this planet," she fumbled, "you have a sun, don't you?"

"A most wonderful sun, from which comes our warmth, and the rays which give us our flowers, our food, our music, and all the things which make life and growth."

"Well," Meg said, "when we are turned toward the sun—our earth, our planet, I mean, toward our sun—we receive its light. And when we're turned away from it, it is night. And if we want to see we have to use artificial lights."

"Artificial lights," the beast sighed. "How very complicated life on your planet must be. Later on you must try to explain some more to me."

"All right," Meg promised, and yet she knew that to try to explain anything that could be seen with the eyes would be impossible, because the beasts in some way saw, knew, understood, far more completely than she, or her parents, or Calvin, or even Charles Wallace.

"Charles Wallace!" she cried. "What are they doing about Charles Wallace? We don't know what IT's doing to him or making him do. Please, oh, please, help us!"

"Yes, yes, little one, of course we will help you. A meeting is in session right now to study what is best to do. We have never before been able to talk to anyone who has managed to escape from a dark planet, so although your father is blaming himself for everything that has happened, we feel that he must be quite an extraordinary person to get out of Camazotz with you at all. But the little boy, and I understand that he is a very special, a very important little boy—ah, my child, you must accept that this will not be easy. To go *back* through the Black Thing, *back* to Camazotz—I don't know. I don't know."

"But Father left him!" Meg said. "He's got to bring him back! He can't just abandon Charles Wallace!"

The beast's communication suddenly became crisp. "Nobody said anything about abandoning anybody. That is not our way. But we know that just because we want something does not mean that we will get what we want, and we still do not know *what* to do. And we cannot allow you, in your present state, to do anything that would jeopardize us all. I can see that you wish your father to go rushing back to Camazotz, and you could probably make him do this, and then where would we be? No. No. You must wait until you are more calm. Now, my darling, here is a robe for you to keep you warm and comfortable." Meg felt herself being lifted again, and a soft, light garment was slipped about her. "Don't worry about your little brother." The tentacles' musical words were soft against her. "We would *never* leave him behind the shadow. But for now you must relax, you must be happy, you must get well."

The gentle words, the feeling that this beast would be able to love her no matter what she said or did, lapped Meg in warmth and peace. She felt a delicate touch of tentacle to her cheek, as tender as her mother's kiss.

"It is so long since my own small ones were grown and gone," the beast said. "You are so tiny and vulnerable. Now I will feed you. You must eat slowly and quietly. I know that you are half starved, that you have been without food far too long, but you must not rush things or you will not get well."

Something completely and indescribably and incredibly delicious was put to Meg's lips, and she swallowed gratefully. With each swallow she felt strength returning to her body, and she realized that she had had nothing to eat since the horrible fake turkey dinner on Camazotz which she had barely tasted. How long ago was her mother's stew? Time no longer had any meaning.

"How long does night last here?" she murmured sleepily. "It will be day again, won't it?"

"Hush," the beast said. "Eat, small one. During the coolness, which is now, we sleep. And, when you waken, there will be warmth again and many things to do. You must eat now, and sleep, and I will stay with you."

"What should I call you, please?" Meg asked.

"Well, now. First, try not to say any words for just a moment. Think within your own mind. Think of all the things you call people, different kinds of people."

While Meg thought, the beast murmured to her gently. "No, *mother* is a special, a one-name; and a father you have here. Not just friend, nor teacher, nor brother, nor sister. What is *acquaintance?* What a funny, hard word. Aunt. Maybe. Yes, perhaps that will do. And you think of such odd words about me. *Thing,* and *monster! Monster,* what a horrid sort of word. I really do not think I am a monster. *Beast.* That will do. *Aunt Beast.*"

"Aunt Beast," Meg murmured sleepily, and laughed.

"Have I said something funny?" Aunt Beast asked in surprise. "Isn't Aunt Beast all right?"

"Aunt Beast is lovely," Meg said. "Please sing to me, Aunt Beast."

If it was impossible to describe sight to Aunt Beast, it would be even more impossible to describe the singing of Aunt Beast to a human being. It was a music even more glorious than the music of the singing creatures on Uriel. It was a music more tangible than form or sight. It had essence and structure. It supported Meg more firmly than the arms of Aunt Beast. It seemed to travel with her, to sweep her aloft in the power of song, so that she was moving in glory among the stars, and for a moment she, too, felt that the words Darkness and Light had no meaning, and only this melody was real.

Meg did not know when she fell asleep within the body of the music. When she wakened Aunt Beast was asleep, too, the softness of her furry, faceless head drooping. Night had gone and a dull gray light filled the room. But she realized now that here on this planet there was no need for color, that the grays and browns merging into each other were not what the beasts knew, and that what she, herself, saw was only the smallest fraction of what the planet was really like. It was she who was limited by her senses, not the blind beasts, for they must have senses of which she could not even dream.

She stirred slightly, and Aunt Beast bent over her immediately, "What a lovely sleep, my darling. Do you feel all right?"

"I feel wonderful," Meg said. "Aunt Beast, what is this planet called?"

"Oh, dear," Aunt Beast sighed. "I find it not easy at all to put things the way your mind shapes them. You call where you came from Camazotz?"

"Well, it's where we came from, but it's not our planet."

"You can call us Ixchel, I guess," Aunt Beast told her. "We share the same sun as lost Camazotz, but that, give thanks, is all we share."

"Are you fighting the Black Thing?" Meg asked.

"Oh, yes," Aunt Beast replied. "In doing that we can never relax. We are called according to His purpose, and whom He calls, them He also justifies. Of course we have help, and without help it would be much more difficult."

"Who helps you?" Meg asked.

"Oh, dear, it is so difficult to explain things to you, small one. And I know now that it is not just because you are a child. The other two are as hard to reach into as you are. What can I tell you that will mean anything to you? Good helps us, the stars help us, perhaps what you would call *light* helps us, love helps us. Oh, my child, I cannot explain! This is something you just have to know or not know."

"But—"

"We look not at the things which are what you would call seen, but at the things which are not seen. For the things which are seen are temporal. But the things which are not seen are eternal."

"Aunt Beast, do you know Mrs. Whatsit?" Meg asked with a sudden flooding of hope.

"Mrs. Whatsit?" Aunt Beast was puzzled. "Oh, child, your language is so utterly simple and limited that it has the effect of extreme complication." Her four arms, tentacles waving, were outflung in a gesture of helplessness. "Would you like me to take you to your father and your Calvin?"

"Oh, yes, please!"

"Let us go, then. They are waiting for you to make plans. And we thought you would enjoy eating—

what is it you call it? oh, yes, breakfast—together. You will be too warm in that heavy fur, now. I will dress you in something lighter, and then we will go."

As though Meg were a baby, Aunt Beast bathed and dressed her, and this new garment, though it was made of a pale fur, was lighter than the lightest summer clothes on earth. Aunt Beast put one tentacled arm about Meg's waist and led her through long, dim corridors in which she could see only shadows of shadows, until they reached a large, columned chamber. Shafts of light came in from an open skylight and converged about a huge, round, stone table. Here were seated several of the great beasts, and Calvin and Mr. Murry, on a stone bench that circled the table. Because the beasts were so tall, even Mr. Murry's feet did not touch the ground, and lanky Calvin's long legs dangled as though he were Charles Wallace. The hall was partially enclosed by vaulted arches leading to long, paved walks. There were no empty walls, no covering roofs, so that although the light was dull in comparison to earth's sunlight, Meg had no feeling of dark or of chill. As Aunt Beast led Meg in, Mr. Murry slid down from the bench and hurried to her, putting his arms about her tenderly.

"They promised us you were all right," he said.

While she had been in Aunt Beast's arms Meg had felt safe and secure. Now her worries about Charles Wallace and her disappointment in her father's human fallibility rose like gorge in her throat.

"I'm fine," she muttered, looking not at Calvin or her father, but at the beasts, for it was to them she turned now for help. It seemed to her that neither her father nor Calvin were properly concerned about Charles Wallace.

"Meg!" Calvin said gaily. "You've never tasted

such food in your life! Come and eat!"

Aunt Beast lifted Meg up onto the bench and sat down beside her, then heaped a plate with food, strange fruits and breads that tasted unlike anything Meg had ever eaten. Everything was dull and colorless and unappetizing to look at, and at first, even remembering the meal Aunt Beast had fed her the night before, Meg hesitated to taste, but once she had managed the first bite she ate eagerly; it seemed that she would never have her fill again.

The others waited until she slowed down. Then Mr. Murry said gravely, "We were trying to work out a plan to rescue Charles Wallace. Since I made such a mistake in tessering away from IT, we feel that it would not be wise for me to try to get back to Camazotz, even alone. If I missed the mark again I could easily get lost and wander forever from galaxy to galaxy, and that would be small help to anyone, least of all to Charles Wallace."

Such a wave of despondency came over Meg that she was no longer able to eat.

"Our friends here," he continued, "feel that it was only the fact that I still wore the glasses your Mrs. Who gave you that kept me within this solar system. Here are the glasses, Meg. But I am afraid that the virtue has gone from them and now they are only glass. Perhaps they were meant to help only once and only on Camazotz. Perhaps it was going through the Black Thing that did it." He pushed the glasses across the table at her.

"These people know about tessering," Calvin gestured at the circle of great beasts, "but they can't do it onto a dark planet."

"Have you tried to call Mrs. Whatsit?" Meg asked.

"Not yet," her father answered.

"But if you haven't thought of anything else, it's the *only* thing to do! Father, don't you care about Charles at all!"

At that Aunt Beast stood up, saying, "Child," in a reproving way. Mr. Murry said nothing, and Meg could see that she had wounded him deeply. She reacted as she would have reacted to Mr. Jenkins. She scowled down at the table, saying, "We've *got* to ask them for help now. You're just stupid if you think we don't."

Aunt Beast spoke to the others. "The child is distraught. Don't judge her harshly. She was almost taken by the Black Thing. Sometimes we can't know what spiritual damage it leaves even when physical recovery is complete."

Meg looked angrily around the table. The beasts sat there, silent, motionless. She felt that she was being measured and found wanting.

Calvin swung away from her and hunched himself up. "Hasn't it occurred to you that we've been trying to tell them about our ladies? What do you think we've been up to all this time? Just stuffing our faces? Okay, you have a shot at it."

"Yes. Try, child." Aunt Beast seated herself again, and pulled Meg up beside her. "But I do not understand this feeling of anger I sense in you. What is it about? There is blame going on, and guilt. Why?"

"Aunt Beast, don't you know?"

"No," Aunt Beast said. "But this is not telling me about—whoever they are you want us to know. Try."

Meg tried. Blunderingly. Fumblingly. At first she described Mrs. Whatsit and her man's coat and multicolored shawls and scarves. Mrs. Who and her white robes and shimmering spectacles, Mrs. Which in her peaked cap and black gown quivering in and out of body. Then she realized that this was absurd. She was describing them only to herself. This wasn't Mrs. Whatsit or Mrs. Who or Mrs. Which. She might as well have described Mrs. Whatsit as she was when she took on the form of a flying creature of Uriel.

"Don't try to use words," Aunt Beast said soothingly. "You're just fighting yourself and me. Think about what they *are*. This *look* doesn't help us at all."

Meg tried again, but she could not get a visual concept out of her mind. She tried to think of Mrs. Whatsit explaining tessering. She tried to think of them in terms of mathematics. Every once in a while she thought she felt a flicker of understanding from Aunt Beast or one of the others, but most of the time all that emanated from them was gentle puzzlement.

"Angels!" Calvin shouted suddenly from across the table. "Guardian angels!" There was a moment's silence, and he shouted again, his face tense with concentration, "Messengers! Messengers of God!"

"I thought for a moment—" Aunt Beast started, then subsided, sighing. "No. It's not clear enough."

"How strange it is that they can't tell us what they themselves seem to know," a tall, thin beast murmured.

One of Aunt Beast's tentacled arms went around Meg's waist again. "They are very young. And on their earth, as they call it, they never communicate with other planets. They revolve about all alone in space."

"Oh," the thin beast said. "Aren't they *lonely*?"

Suddenly a thundering voice reverberated throughout the great hall:

"WWEEE ARRE HHERRE!"

Chapter **12**

THE FOOLISH AND THE WEAK

Meg could see nothing, but she felt her heart pounding with hope. With one accord all the beasts rose to their feet, turned toward one of the arched openings, and bowed their heads and tentacles in greeting. Mrs. Whatsit appeared, standing between two columns. Beside her came Mrs. Who, behind them a quivering of light. The three of them were somehow not quite the same as they had been when Meg had first seen them. Their outlines seemed blurred; colors ran together as in a wet water color painting. But they were there; they were recognizable; they were themselves.

Meg pulled herself away from Aunt Beast, jumped to the floor, and rushed at Mrs. Whatsit. But Mrs. Whatsit held up a warning hand and Meg realized that she was not completely materialized, that she was light and not substance, and embracing her now would have been like trying to hug a sunbeam.

"We had to hurry so there wasn't quite time. . . .

You wanted us?" Mrs. Whatsit asked.

The tallest of the beasts bowed again and took a step away from the table and toward Mrs. Whatsit. "It is a question of the little boy."

"Father left him!" Meg cried. "He left him on Camazotz!"

Appallingly, Mrs. Whatsit's voice was cold. "And what do you expect us to do?"

Meg pressed her knuckles against her teeth so that her braces cut her skin. Then she flung out her arms pleadingly. "But it's Charles Wallace! IT has him, Mrs. Whatsit! Save him, please save him!"

"You know that we can do nothing on Camazotz," Mrs. Whatsit said, her voice still cold.

"You mean you'll let Charles be caught by IT forever?" Meg's voice rose shrilly.

"Did I say that?"

"But we can't do anything! You know we can't! We tried! Mrs. Whatsit, you have to save him!"

"Meg, this is not our way," Mrs. Whatsit said sadly. "I thought you would know that this is not our way."

Mr. Murry took a step forward and bowed, and to Meg's amazement the three ladies bowed back to him. "I don't believe we've been introduced," Mrs. Whatsit said.

"It's Father, you know it's Father." Meg's angry impatience grew. "Father—Mrs. Whatsit, Mrs. Who, and Mrs. Which."

"I'm very glad to—" Mr. Murry mumbled, then went on, "I'm sorry, my glasses are broken, and I can't see you very well."

"It's not necessary to see us," Mrs. Whatsit said.

"If you could teach me enough more about the tesseract so that I could get back to Camazotz—"

"Wwhatt tthenn?" came Mrs. Which's surprising voice.

"I will try to take my child away from IT."

"Annd yyou kknoww tthatt yyou wwill nnott ssucceeedd?"

"There's nothing left except to try."

Mrs. Whatsit spoke gently. "I'm sorry. We cannot allow you to go."

"Then let me," Calvin suggested. "I almost got him away before."

Mrs. Whatsit shook her head. "No, Calvin. Charles has gone even deeper into IT. You will not be permitted to throw yourself in with him, for that, you must realize, is what would happen."

There was a long silence. All the soft rays filtering into the great hall seemed to concentrate on Mrs. Whatsit, Mrs. Who, and the faint light that must be Mrs. Which. No one spoke. One of the beasts moved a tendril slowly back and forth across the stone table top. At last Meg could stand it no longer and she cried out despairingly, "Then what are you going to do? Are you just going to throw Charles away?"

Mrs. Which's voice rolled formidably across the hall. "Ssilencce, cchilldd!"

But Meg could not be silent. She pressed closely against Aunt Beast, but Aunt Beast did not put the protecting tentacles around her. "*I* can't go!" Meg cried. "I can't! You know I can't!"

"Ddidd annybbodyy asskk yyou ttoo?" The grim voice made Meg's skin prickle into gooseflesh.

She burst into tears. She started beating at Aunt Beast like a small child having a tantrum. Her tears rained down her face and spattered Aunt Beast's fur. Aunt Beast stood quietly against the assault.

"All right, I'll go!" Meg sobbed. "I know you want me to go!"

"We want nothing from you that you do without grace," Mrs. Whatsit said, "or that you do without understanding."

Meg's tears stopped as abruptly as they had started. "But I do understand." She felt tired and unexpectedly peaceful. Now the coldness that, under Aunt Beast's ministrations, had left her body had also left her mind. She looked toward her father and her confused anger was gone and she felt only love and pride. She smiled at him, asking forgiveness, and then pressed up against Aunt Beast. This time Aunt Beast's arm went around her.

Mrs. Which's voice was grave. "Wwhatt ddoo yyou unndderrsstanndd?"

"That it has to be me. It can't be anyone else. I don't understand Charles, but he understands me. I'm the one who's closest to him. Father's been away for so long, since Charles Wallace was a baby. They don't know each other. And Calvin's only known Charles for such a little time. If it had been longer then he would have been the one, but—oh, I see, I see, I understand, it has to be me. There isn't anyone else."

Mr. Murry, who had been sitting, his elbows on his knees, his chin on his fists, rose. "I will not allow it!"

"Wwhyy?" Mrs. Which demanded.

"Look, I don't know what or who you are, and at this point I don't care. I will not allow my daughter to go alone into this danger."

"Wwhyy?"

"You know what the outcome will probably be! And she's weak now, weaker than she was before. She was almost killed by the Black Thing. I fail to understand how you can even consider such a thing."

Calvin jumped down. "Maybe IT's right about you! Or maybe you're in league with IT. *I'm* the one to go if anybody goes! Why did you bring me along at all? To take care of Meg! You said so yourself!"

"But you have done that," Mrs. Whatsit assured him.

"I haven't done anything!" Calvin shouted. "You can't send Meg! I won't allow it! I'll put my foot down! I won't permit it!"

"Don't you see that you're making something that is already hard for Meg even harder?" Mrs. Whatsit asked him.

Aunt Beast turned tentacles toward Mrs. Whatsit. "Is she strong enough to tesser again? You know what she has been through."

"If Which takes her she can manage," Mrs. Whatsit said.

"If it will help I could go too, and hold her." Aunt Beast's arm around Meg tightened.

"Oh, Aunt Beast—" Meg started.

But Mrs. Whatsit cut her off. "No."

"I was afraid not," Aunt Beast said humbly. "I just wanted you to know that I *would.*"

"Mrs.—uh—Whatsit." Mr. Murry frowned and pushed his hair back from his face. Then he shoved with his middle finger at his nose as though he were trying to get spectacles closer to his eyes. "Are you remembering that she is only a child?"

"And she's backward," Calvin bellowed.

"I resent that," Meg said hotly, hoping that indignation would control her trembling. "I'm better than you at math and you know it."

"Do you have the courage to go alone?" Mrs. Whatsit asked her.

Meg's voice was flat. "No. But it doesn't matter." She turned to her father and Calvin. "You know it's the only thing to do. You know they'd never send me alone if—"

"How do we know they're not in league with IT?" Mr. Murry demanded.

"Father!"

"No, Meg," Mrs. Whatsit said. "I do not blame your father for being angry and suspicious and frightened. And I cannot pretend that we are doing anything but sending you into the gravest kind of danger. I have to acknowledge quite openly that it may be a fatal danger. I know this. But I do not believe it. And the Happy Medium doesn't believe it, either."

"Can't she see what's going to happen?" Calvin asked.

"Oh, not in this kind of thing." Mrs. Whatsit sounded surprised at his question. "If we knew ahead of time what was going to happen we'd be— we'd be like the people on Camazotz, with no lives of our own, with everything all planned and done for us. How can I explain it to you? Oh, I know. In your language you have a form of poetry called the sonnet."

"Yes, yes," Calvin said impatiently. "What's that got to do with the Happy Medium?"

"Kindly pay me the courtesy of listening to me." Mrs. Whatsit's voice was stern, and for a moment Calvin stopped pawing the ground like a nervous colt. "It is a very strict form of poetry, is it not?"

"Yes."

"There are fourteen lines, I believe, all in iambic pentameter. That's a very strict rhythm or meter, yes?"

"Yes." Calvin nodded.

"And each line has to end with a rigid rhyme pattern. And if the poet does not do it exactly this way, it is not a sonnet, is it?"

"No."

"But within this strict form the poet has complete freedom to say whatever he wants, doesn't he?"

"Yes." Calvin nodded again.

"So," Mrs. Whatsit said.

"So what?"

"Oh, do not be stupid, boy!" Mrs. Whatsit scolded. "You know perfectly well what I am driving at!"

"You mean you're comparing our lives to a sonnet? A strict form, but freedom within it?"

"Yes," Mrs. Whatsit said. "You're given the form, but you have to write the sonnet yourself. What you say is completely up to you."

"Please," Meg said. "Please. If I've got to go I want to go and get it over with. Each minute you put it off makes it harder."

"Sshee iss rrightt," boomed Mrs. Which's voice. "Itt iss ttime."

"You may say goodbye." Mrs. Whatsit was giving her not permission, but a command.

Meg curtsied clumsily to the beasts. "Thank you all. Very much. I know you saved my life." She did not add what she could not help thinking: Saved it for what? So that IT could get me?

She put her arms about Aunt Beast, pressed up against the soft, fragrant fur. "Thank you," she whispered. "I love you."

"And I you, little one." Aunt Beast pressed gentle tendrils against Meg's face.

"Cal—" Meg said, holding out her hand.

Calvin came to her and took her hand, then drew her roughly to him and kissed her. He didn't say anything, and he turned away before he had a chance to see the surprised happiness that brightened Meg's eyes.

At last she turned to her father. "I'm—I'm sorry, Father."

He took both her hands in his, bent down to her with his short-sighted eyes. "Sorry for what, Megatron?"

Tears almost came to her eyes at the gentle use of the old nickname. "I wanted you to do it all for me. I wanted everything to be all easy and simple. . . . So I tried to pretend that it was all your fault . . . because I was scared, and I didn't want to have to do anything myself—"

"But I wanted to do it for you," Mr. Murry said. "That's what every parent wants." He looked into her dark, frightened eyes. "I won't let you go, Meg. I am going."

"No." Mrs. Whatsit's voice was sterner than Meg had ever heard it. "You are going to allow Meg the privilege of accepting this danger. You are a wise man, Mr. Murry. You are going to let her go."

Mr. Murry sighed. He drew Meg close to him. "Little Megaparsec. Don't be afraid. We will try to have courage for you. That is all we can do. Your mother—"

"Mother was always shoving me out in the world," Meg said. "She'd want me to do this. You know she would. Tell her—" she started, choked, then held up her head and said, "No. Never mind. I'll tell her myself."

"Good girl. Of course you will."

Now Meg walked slowly around the great table to where Mrs. Whatsit was still poised between the columns. "Are you going with me?"

"No. Only Mrs. Which."

"The Black Thing—" Fear made her voice tremble. "When Father tessered me through it, it almost got me."

"Your father is singularly inexperienced," Mrs. Whatsit said, "though a fine man, and worth teaching. At the moment he still treats tessering as though he were working with a machine. We will not let the Black Thing get you. I don't think."

This was not exactly comforting.

The momentary vision and faith that had come to Meg dwindled. "But suppose I can't get Charles Wallace away from IT—"

"Stop." Mrs. Whatsit held up her hand. "We gave you gifts the last time we took you to Camazotz. We will not let you go empty-handed this time. But what we can give you now is nothing you can touch with your hands. I give you my love, Meg. Never forget that. My love always."

Mrs. Who, eyes shining behind spectacles, beamed at Meg. Meg felt in her blazer pocket and handed back the spectacles she had used on Camazotz.

"Your father is right." Mrs. Who took the spectacles and hid them somewhere in the folds of her robes. "The virtue is gone from them. And what I have to give you this time you must try to understand not word by word, but in a flash, as you understand the tesseract. Listen, Meg. Listen well. *The foolishness of God is wiser than men; and the weakness of God is stronger than men. For ye see your calling, brethren, how that not many wise men after the flesh, not many mighty, not many noble, are called, but God hath chosen the foolish things of the world to confound the wise; and God hath chosen the weak things of the world to confound the things which are mighty. And base things of the world, and things which are despised, hath God chosen, yea, and things which are not, to bring to nought things that are.*" She paused, and then she said, "May the right prevail." Her spectacles seemed to flicker. Behind her, through her, one of the columns became visible. There was a final gleam from the glasses, and she was gone. Meg looked nervously to where Mrs. Whatsit had been standing before Mrs. Who spoke. But Mrs. Whatsit was no longer there.

"No!" Mr. Murry cried, and stepped toward Meg.

Mrs. Which's voice came through her shimmer. "I ccannnott hholldd yyourr hanndd, chilldd."

Immediately Meg was swept into darkness, into nothingness, and then into the icy devouring cold of the Black Thing. Mrs. Which won't let it get me, she thought over and over while the cold of the Black Thing seemed to crunch at her bones.

Then they were through it, and she was standing breathlessly on her feet on the same hill on which they had first landed on Camazotz. She was cold and a little numb, but no worse than she had often been in the winter in the country when she had spent an afternoon skating on the pond. She looked around. She was completely alone. Her heart began to pound.

Then, seeming to echo from all around her, came Mrs. Which's unforgettable voice. "I hhave nnott ggivenn yyou mmy ggifftt. *Yyou hhave ssomethinngg thatt ITT hhass nnott.* Thiss ssomethinngg iss yyourr onlly wweapponn. Bbutt yyou mmusstt ffinndd itt fforr yyourrssellff." Then the voice ceased, and Meg knew that she was alone.

She walked slowly down the hill, her heart thumping painfully against her ribs. There below her was the same row of identical houses they had seen before, and beyond these the linear buildings of the city. She walked along the quiet street. It was dark and the street was deserted. No children playing ball or skipping rope. No mother figures at the doors. No father figures returning from work. In the same window of each house was a light, and as Meg walked down the street all the lights were extinguished simultaneously. Was it because of her presence, or was it simply that it was time for lights out?

She felt numb, beyond rage or disappointment or even fear. She put one foot ahead of the other with precise regularity, not allowing her pace to lag. She was not thinking; she was not planning; she was simply walking slowly but steadily toward the city and the domed building where IT lay.

Now she approached the outlying buildings of the city. In each of them was a vertical line of light, but it was a dim, eerie light, not the warm light of stairways in cities at home. And there were no isolated brightly lit windows where someone was working late, or an office was being cleaned. Out of each building came one man, perhaps a watchman, and each man started walking the width of the building. They appeared not to see her. At any rate they paid no attention to her whatsoever, and she went on past them.

What have I got that IT hasn't got? she thought suddenly. What have I possibly got?

Now she was walking by the tallest of the business buildings. More dim vertical lines of light. The walls glowed slightly to give a faint illumination to the streets. CENTRAL Central Intelligence was ahead of her. Was the man with red eyes still sitting there? Or was he allowed to go to bed? But this was not where she must go, though the man with red eyes seemed the kind old gentleman he claimed to be when compared with IT. But he was no longer of any consequence in the search for Charles Wallace. She must go directly to IT.

IT isn't used to being resisted. Father said that's how he managed, and how Calvin and I managed as long as we did. Father saved me then. There's nobody here to save me now. I have to do it myself. I have to resist IT by myself. Is that what I have that IT hasn't got? No, I'm sure IT can resist. IT just isn't used to having *other* people resist.

CENTRAL Central Intelligence blocked with its huge rectangle the end of the square. She turned to walk around it, and almost imperceptibly her steps slowed.

It was not far to the great dome which housed IT.

I'm going to Charles Wallace. That's what's important. That's what I have to think of. I wish I could feel numb again the way I did at first. Suppose IT has him somewhere else? Suppose he isn't there?

I have to go there first, anyhow. That's the only way I can find out.

Her steps got slower and slower as she passed the great bronzed doors, the huge slabs of the CENTRAL Central Intelligence building, as she finally saw ahead of her the strange, light, pulsing dome of IT.

Father said it was all right for me to be afraid. He said to go ahead and be afraid. And Mrs. Who said—I don't understand what she said but I think it was meant to make me not hate being only me, and me being the way I am. And Mrs. Whatsit said to remember that she loves me. That's what I have to think about. Not about being afraid. Or not as smart as IT. Mrs. Whatsit loves me. That's quite something, to be loved by someone like Mrs. Whatsit.

She was there.

No matter how slowly her feet had taken her at the end, they had taken her there.

Directly ahead of her was the circular building, its walls glowing with violet flame, its silvery roof pulsing with a light that seemed to Meg to be insane. Again she could feel the light, neither warm nor cold, but reaching out to touch her, pulling her toward IT.

There was a sudden sucking, and she was within.

It was as though the wind had been knocked out of her. She gasped for breath, for breath in her own rhythm, not the permeating pulsing of IT. She could feel the inexorable beat within her body, controlling her heart, her lungs.

But not herself. Not Meg. It did not quite have her.

She blinked her eyes rapidly and against the rhythm until the redness before them cleared and she could see. There was the brain, there was IT, lying pulsing and quivering on the dais, soft and exposed and nauseating. Charles Wallace was crouched beside IT, his eyes still slowly twirling, his jaw still slack, as she had seen him before, with a tic in his forehead reiterating the revolting rhythm of IT.

As she saw him it was again as though she had been punched in the stomach, for she had to realize afresh that she was seeing Charles, and yet it was not Charles at all. Where was Charles Wallace, her own beloved Charles Wallace?

What is it I have got that IT hasn't got?

"You have nothing that IT hasn't got," Charles Wallace said coldly. "How nice to have you back, dear sister. We have been waiting for you. We knew that Mrs. Whatsit would send you. She is our friend, you know."

For an appalling moment Meg believed, and in that moment she felt her brain being gathered up into IT.

"No!" she screamed at the top of her lungs. "No! You lie!"

For a moment she was free from IT's clutches again.

As long as I can stay angry enough IT can't get me. Is that what I have that IT doesn't have?

"Nonsense," Charles Wallace said. "You have nothing that IT doesn't have."

"You're lying," she replied, and she felt only anger toward this boy who was not Charles Wallace at all. No, it was not anger, it was loathing; it was hatred, sheer and unadulterated, and as she became lost in hatred she also began to be lost in IT. The red miasma swam before her eyes; her stomach churned in IT's rhythm. Her body trembled with the strength of her hatred and the strength of IT.

With the last vestige of consciousness she jerked her mind and body. Hate was nothing that IT didn't have. IT knew all about hate.

"You are lying about that, and you were lying about Mrs. Whatsit!" she screamed.

"Mrs. Whatsit hates you," Charles Wallace said.

And that was where IT made IT's fatal mistake, for as Meg said, automatically, "Mrs. Whatsit loves me; that's what she told me, that she loves me," suddenly she knew.

She knew!

Love.

That was what she had that IT did not have.

She had Mrs. Whatsit's love, and her father's, and her mother's, and the real Charles Wallace's love, and the twins', and Aunt Beast's.

And she had her love for them.

But how could she use it? What was she meant to do?

If she could give love to IT perhaps it would shrivel up and die, for she was sure that IT could not withstand love. But she, in all her weakness and foolishness and baseness and nothingness, was incapable of loving IT. Perhaps it was not too much to ask of her, but she could not do it.

But she could love Charles Wallace.

She could stand there and she could love Charles Wallace.

Her own Charles Wallace, the real Charles Wallace, the child for whom she had come back to Camazotz, to IT, the baby who was so much more than she was, and who was yet so utterly vulnerable.

She could love Charles Wallace.

Charles. Charles, I love you. My baby brother who always takes care of me. Come back to me, Charles Wallace, come away from IT, come back, come home. I love you, Charles. Oh, Charles Wallace, I love you.

Tears were streaming down her cheeks, but she was unaware of them.

Now she was even able to look at him, at this animated thing that was not her own Charles Wallace at all. She was able to look and love.

I love you. Charles Wallace, you are my darling and my dear and the light of my life and the treasure of my heart. I love you. I love you. I love you.

Slowly his mouth closed. Slowly his eyes stopped their twirling. The tic in the forehead ceased its revolting twitch. Slowly he advanced toward her.

"I love you!" she cried. "I love you, Charles! I love you!"

Then suddenly he was running, pelting, he was in her arms, he was shrieking with sobs. "Meg! Meg! Meg!"

"I love you, Charles!" she cried again, her sobs almost as loud as his, her tears mingling with his. "I love you! I love you! I love you!"

A whirl of darkness. An icy cold blast. An angry, resentful howl that seemed to tear through her. Darkness again. Through the darkness to save her came a sense of Mrs. Whatsit's presence, so that she knew it could not be IT who now had her in its clutches.

And then the feel of earth beneath her, of something in her arms, and she was rolling over on the sweet smelling autumnal earth, and Charles Wallace was crying out, "Meg! Oh, Meg!"

Now she was hugging him close to her, and his little arms were clasped tightly about her neck.

"Meg, you saved me! You saved me!" he said over and over.

"Meg!" came a call, and there were her father and Calvin hurrying through the darkness toward them.

Still holding Charles she struggled to stand up and look around. "Father! Cal! Where are we?"

Charles Wallace, holding her hand tightly, was looking around, too, and suddenly he laughed, his own, sweet, contagious laugh. "In the twins' vegetable garden! And we landed in the broccoli!"

Meg began to laugh, too, at the same time that she was trying to hug her father, to hug Calvin, and not to let go of Charles Wallace for one second.

"Meg, you did it!" Calvin shouted. "You saved Charles!"

"I'm very proud of you, my daughter." Mr. Murry kissed her gravely, then turned toward the house. "Now I must go in to Mother." Meg could tell that he was trying to control his anxiety and eagerness.

"Look!" she pointed to the house, and there were the twins and Mrs. Murry walking toward them through the long, wet grass.

"First thing tomorrow I must get some new glasses," Mr. Murry said, squinting in the moonlight, and then starting to run toward his wife.

Dennys' voice came crossly over the lawn. "Hey, Meg, it's bedtime."

Sandy suddenly yelled, "Father!"

Mr. Murry was running across the lawn, Mrs. Murry running toward him, and they were in each other's arms, and then there was a tremendous happy jumble of arms and legs and hugging, the older Murrys and Meg and Charles Wallace and the twins, and Calvin grinning by them until Meg reached out and pulled him in and Mrs. Murry gave him a special hug all of his own. They were talking and laughing all at once, when they were startled by a crash, and Fortinbras, who could bear being left out of the happiness not one second longer, catapulted his sleek black body right through the screened door to the kitchen. He dashed across the lawn to join in the joy, and almost knocked them all over with the exuberance of his greeting.

Meg knew all at once that Mrs. Whatsit, Mrs. Who, and Mrs. Which must be near, because all through her she felt a flooding of joy and of love that was even greater and deeper than the joy and love which were already there.

She stopped laughing and listened, and Charles listened, too. "Hush."

Then there was a whirring, and Mrs. Whatsit, Mrs. Who, and Mrs. Which were standing in front of them, and the joy and love were so tangible that Meg felt that if she only knew where to reach she could touch it with her bare hands.

Mrs. Whatsit said breathlessly, "Oh, my darlings, I'm sorry we don't have time to say goodbye to you properly. You see, we have to—"

But they never learned what it was that Mrs. Whatsit, Mrs. Who, and Mrs. Which had to do, for there was a gust of wind, and they were gone.

RELATED READINGS

Odd Jobs

by Judith Gorog

*Miss Hetty, Miss Letty, and Miss Netty.
Mrs. Whatsit, Mrs. Who, and Mrs. Which.
Do these beings resemble each other in
ways besides their names? What other
connections do you find between this
story and the novel?*

Miss Hetty cleared her throat and began to speak. "Our brother, who, unfortunately, is away on a trip . . ."

Miss Letty giggled. Miss Netty gave her a hard look, and Miss Hetty continued.

"Perhaps I should add that you were not the first teenagers we hired through the Youth Employment Service, but we had despaired of finding anyone who could assist us.

"You see, we need something more than just the help one would expect to provide three old ladies living in a large old house. There are those tasks, of course, and you have done splendidly. But you two have qualities about you that make me think that you can provide the assistance we truly need, which is something more.

"Our brother left us a series of puzzles, little tasks to be done. It was, well, a prank, a series of jokes on us. I'm afraid he was a bit annoyed with us for some little jokes we played on him. I should add that when these pranks began, we were all quite a bit younger than we are now." She looked at John and Jane, then continued.

"One reason we needed the cleaning you have

done was so that we could look carefully for any clues or messages he might have left us in any of those storage areas you so beautifully tidied up for us."

John nearly groaned aloud at the thought. Every time he and Jane had got something straightened out, one of the three elderly sisters would begin to rummage through the stuff just one more time.

"Surely," continued Miss Hetty, "you can help us now?"

John looked at Jane, then shrugged his assent.

Jane was having a terrible time concentrating on what Miss Hetty was saying. That music, wild and sad—someone must be playing some sort of flute or reed. It was always here in the old ladies' house, but now it was so loud that Jane could barely sit still. How could the others not hear it? She wondered if she was cracking up. Jane looked around her. Miss Hetty was waiting for an answer.

"Oh yes, yes. I think we can help. At least we can try," Jane finally stammered.

She must ask John about the music. It seemed the minute she left the place she always forgot, except that lately she had begun to hear it in her head at odd times during the day and night. Beautiful tune, so sad.

Miss Hetty continued. "One task is to decipher a verse and then to do what it says. It was given in Greek, not that it matters particularly, and then in wretched German doggerel."

"And the English is nearly as bad," interjected Miss Letty.

"True," replied Miss Hetty. "Here it is."

Wait for the silver, and you'll miss the gold;
Fail this year and the increase is hundred-fold.

For a minute, everyone looked at everyone else in silence. Finally, Jane asked, although she was never sure why, "Would you mind saying it in Greek? It won't help us to understand, but I'd just like to hear it."

Miss Hetty read, and Jane's future was set.

Of the twins, John was the one who was all eyes for seeing the world and hands for drawing it. His notebook margins and every scrap of paper he touched were filled with drawings. At track meets he had driven the coach to distraction his first season with that sketch pad. Except for when he was warming up or actually in an event, John drew all the time. Coach had opposed the sketching as "too much use of small muscles, with too much concentration." But when John set records and won meets, Coach relaxed.

Jane clearly had an ear for music, for languages, for people's accents, and for their stories. She wasn't sure how she would put her talents to work, for she played the piano as much for escape as for pleasure in making music, and she often felt she read without much discrimination simply because the books were there. Now the language of that puzzle captured her completely.

The twins left the house, promising the old ladies that they would come back as soon as they had some ideas about the puzzle. No, it wouldn't be tomorrow. They had to do some work at home. April was hot this year and everything in the garden was rushing into bloom.

For a few blocks they walked without talking.

"Money in the bank increases from year to year," muttered Jane, "but so would golden daffodils or tulips in the garden." She gestured toward the flowers along the way, petals now closed for the night.

John nodded. He wondered whether Jane had thought of money for the same reason he had. They were nearly home. He had already begun to hope that Aunt Nasturtium's car would not be in the driveway. Lately she had had a most unsettling habit of arriving to check on them whenever the old ladies had not paid the twins for more than a few days. The old ladies needed them nearly every day after school, but they paid them at odd intervals.

Aunt Nasturtium was their father's sister. She saw it as her mission in life to drive Daddy to "success." Every visit brought a lecture on how their father surely would get his reward in Heaven, since he certainly wasn't getting it on earth. Each birthday, every Christmas, produced a book that declared that success demanded this or that generally unscrupulous practice, outlined what to do and how to do it, and had quizzes at the end of every chapter. Daddy said, "Thank you," and never opened a single one. Lately Aunt Nasturtium seemed to be turning her attention toward Jane and John.

"Whew," John sighed.

"She's not there," observed Jane with obvious relief. "It doesn't explain the silver," she said, returning to the puzzle, "but then money can be silver, too."

"I don't know," John shrugged. "I'm too hungry to think. Who is cook tonight? Dad?"

In a town where everyone was named Candace, Kimberly, Hardy, or Meredith, it was hard to be named Jane and John, and to be twins at that. It was as if their parents had been too surprised at getting two of them to do much about calling them something a bit less, well, ordinary. John had once wondered aloud whether having a sister named Nasturtium had perhaps prejudiced their father, at least against anything but the very simplest of names.

Then when they were in the eighth grade, Mother had died. Daddy, bless him, had successfully resisted Aunt Nasturtium's offer to move in with them. Her frequent visits, however, were to be endured.

The next morning Jane and John set to work on the things they had neglected at home while they had been working for the three old ladies on Hawthorne Terrace. They cleaned the garage and the shed, then cut and trimmed the grass.

Jane found herself repeating the puzzle verse while she dug. "Wait for the silver, and you'll miss the gold." With a certain satisfaction, she set to work on the dandelions. They used their mother's old tactic: "Every day take out the ones that have flowered. Then you'll clear the lawn. Do it every year and the dandelions never take over, though some will always blow onto the lawn from somewhere else and reseed themselves." This system of taking them out was much less discouraging than to be assigned the job: dig out *all* the dandelions!

Although Jane followed her mother's dictum, she sometimes also took out a green dandelion plant near one in flower. Getting ahead of them that way made her feel she'd tricked them and gave her a small triumph.

Jane dug viciously at a plantain. These were tougher birds than the dandelions. The dandelion root was long and slim, easy to pry out, but the plantain root went tenaciously in every direction.

"Never saw a flower on these wretched things. Can't eat them. Wonder what use they are," she gritted through her teeth as she attacked another one.

"John! I think I've got it!" she yelped. Then, feeling silly, she looked around to see if anyone else had heard her.

"What?" he brushed the sweat from his forehead. "Dandelions are gold . . ."

"Sure! Then silver, and if you don't dig them out, it sure is a hundred-, maybe a thousand-fold." Then he groaned. "Have you noticed the lawn at the old ladies' house? It will take us weeks to clear it."

"Goody," Jane responded without much enthusiasm. She sighed. "At least it's out of doors, better than cleaning closets and attics."

"Yeah," John replied. "But why did their brother make a puzzle out of it? Why not just leave them a note to weed the lawn?"

"Funny about dandelions," John said later. "Once, up in the Adirondacks, I came out of the cabin, must have been May, early spring up there. The ground was still kinda bare, so I really noticed a pretty yellow flower in the clearing. I thought, gee, that's nice, too early for Indian paintbrush though, and never saw a yellow one. When I went over to see, it was a dandelion, very thin, with just one flower, three long leaves, not a single green bud showing below on the ground. All alone there on the brown grass it was beautiful. I always liked them after that." He paused. "Until tomorrow, when we start the old ladies' lawn."

The next day when the twins reported their solution to the puzzle, the three ladies were strangely unresponsive. Finally Miss Hetty recovered herself and smiled at them.

"Thank you. It will be a miserable job for you, and I am sorry. We had hoped that the solution to the puzzle would be somewhat . . . somewhat more helpful to us." She turned away. "Thank you. Please let me know how long it takes you to do it so we can pay you accordingly."

It took several days. By the time the twins were

finished with the job, the rains came. April had been the last month of a long drought. Now May brought four weeks of rain. And when the rains came, the old ladies disappeared. Jane and John reported for work to find only notes for them in a silent, empty house.

Silent for the most part, that is; silent except for the music, which Jane heard less often now. It was always faint, sometimes so faint that she strained to hear it.

Gone, too, was the characteristic smell of the house, the one Jane had tried unsuccessfully to identify. It was pleasant, fresh, but not like air fresheners—they made Jane sneeze. No, this was a smell she should know; one she did know, but couldn't name. It hadn't seemed to belong there. Now it was gone.

The twins went to the old ladies' house as often as they could. In the house they found notes, but not the old ladies. The notes rarely requested work, and never included any payment; they did, however, give permission to use the library in the house. Working there was useful. Jane and John got a great deal of studying done and they could avoid a good number of Aunt Nasturtium's visits.

She never let up. How would they pay for college? How could they continue to work for three old ladies who paid them so erratically? Where *were* the old ladies? Aunt Nasturtium threatened to go to the head of the Youth Employment Service.

Then she was off on a new tack. The twins should be with young people more. They should study more—or less, depending on her mood. Daddy was used to her; he could take it without getting mad. The twins had not yet developed that talent.

The old-fashioned library was a pleasant refuge. Its shelves went from floor to ceiling and were crammed with books, except for a single shelf of large conch shells. The long library table in the center of the room had three good reading lamps, piles of books, and an enormous glass jar with a heavy glass stopper, the kind they had in groceries a hundred years ago. The jar was full of small seashells. John had already drawn it, and some of the large shells, and the room, and the few old fragments of vases and amphorae, and the old ladies as well.

He drew Jane while she read. His sketch pads filled rapidly. Those pads were just one more reason they needed to be paid for their work. They tried never to hit Dad for money. After their mother's long illness, he had plenty to pay for as it was.

So when the old ladies neglected to pay them, it *was* inconvenient, but John and Jane had grown fond of them. Besides, it was awful to have Aunt Nasty always be right. Instead of facing her, the twins escaped to the cool old house to read and draw.

"I wonder if Miss Hetty used to be a professor of, say, Greek literature," mused Jane one evening. "So many books in Greek, and on Greek literature, on Greece. It's like being turned loose on a feast."

"Then Miss Netty, with her husky voice and her purple dresses, was probably an art history professor, I'd say," added John, hoisting a large tome. "I've never seen such beautiful stuff."

"And Miss Letty?" Jane looked up. "Poor thing. Everything she touches spills and drops. She always complains about 'this' body. Sometimes, when she is still, though, she's as beautiful, as graceful as a dancer in repose, or like one of these." She touched a fragment of a vase on which was painted the silhouette of an acrobat. "Maybe she was a dancer and was sick or injured."

"Funny," added John, "she did say once when she

spilled something how she had not always been like this. But that is the only reference any of them has ever made to the past, their past. They are full of stories about—" John stopped. "What's the matter?"

Jane had started out of her chair.

"What?" insisted John.

"It's stopped," whispered Jane.

"What's stopped?"

"The music. It broke off without finishing. It often grows faint, but it always finishes. Lately it has been faint. Sometimes it used to be really loud."

"*What* music?" asked John, looking around the room.

"Oh. It drives me wild. I keep meaning to ask you or the ladies whether you hear it, but I always seem to forget or something interrupts me. Then I hear it here," she tapped her forehead. "It's a sad, lonely song, played on some sort of flute. It has lots of variations, but always the same theme. Sometimes it's very loud, but lately it's been so faint, I find myself straining to hear it. Now it stopped in the middle, just like that."

"Music, empty house, nutty old ladies. . . . Let's go home. I'm starved. Never did see any food here," said John, gathering up his pad, books, and pencils.

"Me neither. Where can the old ladies be? All the time we've known them they have never once gone out shopping, to doctors, dentists, on visits, nothing you'd expect three old ladies to do. So why should they leave when it rains? When they come back I will ask them about the music, first thing."

She slammed her books together. John locked the door behind them. Jane was hungry, too. She forgot to ask John about the smell.

In June, the sun reappeared with sudden intensity. The world became dry, limp with heat. On the first day of sunshine, Jane went directly to Hawthorne Terrace after school. The minute she let herself in the front door, she knew that the ladies were back in the house. Jane stopped in the hall. The smell had returned. It was overpowering and confusing because it shouldn't have been there. Then suddenly she knew: it smelled like the ocean. She almost expected the wind to blow. But why? And how? The ocean was several hours away by car.

The music started up again. Jane listened to it, feeling such overwhelming sadness that she thought she would weep. She listened so intently that a few minutes passed before she realized she was eavesdropping on a quarrel.

Miss Netty and Miss Letty were both talking at once, both very angry. Then Miss Hetty was lecturing her sisters in firm, measured sentences.

"It is no use finding fault with one another. Our brother tricked us into assuming human shape, here so far from the sea, and now we must complete the tasks so that he will release us. We are nearly done. Please do not quarrel. These mortal twins are helping us." She sighed. "I do admit that I am disturbed, too. Where is our brother hiding to watch us suffer here? Has this not gone on too long? We are aging in these human shapes."

At that Miss Letty began to sob. "Like poor Tithonus, we'll become dried-up little crickets."

Miss Hetty's voice grew gentler. "Ah, don't cry, dear. The rains did make it possible for us to return to the sea for a short time. That was a gift. Now, don't cry. I know that we are nearly done."

Jane slipped out as quietly as she could. The music wailed behind her.

John had started home but had seen Aunt Nasturtium's car and turned back, trying to decide whether to go to school, to the public library, or to Hawthorne Terrace. With a shrug for Aunt Nasturtium, he headed for the house on Hawthorne Terrace. He would ask the old ladies about that music Jane kept hearing. Instead, he found Miss Letty standing in the living room weeping. The floor and the furniture were covered with a thick layer of straight pins.

"Box explode?" asked John sympathetically.

"May as well have," whimpered Miss Letty. "Why, why, why is my brother so mean? I'll never get all of them picked up. They keep spilling again and again. Day after day it is the same."

John tried not to stare. For a minute she looked like a little child standing there.

"I'll get something to pick them up," he reassured her. "Wait here; I'll be right back."

He rushed out the door and ran home. With a brief "Hi, sorry, gotta rush" to Aunt Nasturtium, he was in and out of his room and back at Hawthorne Terrace.

Miss Hetty came in just as he swept the large bar magnet once more over the floor. This time there was not a single pin on the bar. John looked carefully. The floor was clean. Cautiously, holding her breath, Miss Letty handed Miss Hetty the full, closed box.

"Done!" cried Miss Hetty. "That was one I feared you'd never do." She turned to John. "Thank you. We are nearly done with our tasks. There is just one more."

"One impossible one," said Miss Netty as she came into the room. "It is something for Heracles."

"The task," continued Miss Hetty, "is to draw a team of four horses and a cart from New York to Philadelphia in one passage of the sun through the skies."

"Meaning sunup to sundown?" asked John.

"I suppose so," replied Miss Hetty, "but—"

John chuckled. "I can do it tomorrow, Saturday, easily."

The ladies looked bewildered. John left without explaining.

It was late that night before Jane had a chance to tell John what she had overheard. "Even knowing more about who they are, or what they are, doesn't help us to help them. They sounded so miserable. Even if the music didn't tear me up, I'd still feel sorry for them."

"Well," John yawned. "Let's see if I can do the last job for them tomorrow. And you can ask about the music."

Jane nodded. "Then we can tell them what we know. We'll see."

John returned late the next day, triumphantly bearing a large sketch pad. "Four people offered to buy it," he grinned.

Miss Hetty, Miss Letty, and Miss Netty crowded around. Jane watched.

"See? I drew a four-horse team pulling a chariot, which seemed more attractive than a mere farm cart. I drew it all the way from New York to Philadelphia, on the train. Does that do?"

Proper Miss Hetty whooped for joy. "Now we must be done! We did most of our brother's silly tasks and you two, thank you, have done the rest. I thought he would be here to watch our struggle. For some reason he has hidden from us. Now he can come back. Where is he?" she demanded in a voice that rang through the silent house. "He *must* come and set us free!"

The three ladies looked around. No one came. In the silence that followed, Miss Letty began to cry without a sound. Jane heard the music start up again, faint, slow, so incredibly sad. All three ladies looked broken, weary, old.

"That music," Jane whispered. "Can't anyone hear it?"

"Music?" repeated Miss Netty.

"It sounds like this but it's played on a flute or pipes of some sort." Jane opened the piano and began to play along with the music she had heard so many times.

All three sisters stared at Jane in horror.

"Is this another trick?" whispered Miss Hetty.

"Oh, no!" interrupted Miss Letty. "I remember now! I hid our brother's pipes. Then when I learned that he had tricked us and trapped us, I was so upset that I forgot."

She ran to the jar of seashells and removed the stopper. It took both hands to lift the jar. Miss Letty poured the shells out onto the table. "I must have surprised him in his own flute," she murmured. In the middle of the soft pastels of the seashells lay double panpipes of wood or reed.

Jane wasn't sure what she saw next—a flash of curved leg, of hoof, then a man in elegant, rather old-fashioned clothes standing in the doorway as if he had been there watching them for quite a few minutes. He was pale and a bit worn, but handsome.

"We have had enough of jokes, haven't we?" he asked.

All three sisters rushed to him.

"Indeed we have," sighed Miss Hetty. "Now we can go home."

"You must be patient a bit longer and wait for rain," he replied.

Miss Letty groaned. Her face still glistened with tears. Her brother gently patted her hand.

"You have my promise. You will soon be home. Someone clearly has taken pity on us all or else you would not have had the help of these twins, and this little adventure, which has gone on for too long, might never have ended." He bowed most formally to Jane and John. "Thank you. Before we leave, we must give you your payment." Miss Hetty went to her desk and took out a rather large leather purse.

"Here it is," she said, pulling out one bill after another. "Here is payment for all those hours for which you have not yet been paid. That, too, was part of our task, to find someone willing to help us even when we did not pay as regularly as we ought. We had been silly and selfish for so long with our constant tricks and jokes, and our jealousy of our brother's freedom to come and go as he wished, on sea or land, that he decided to teach us a lesson."

"But our brother, too, was caught," added Miss Letty.

"If I am not being too inquisitive," said Jane, tentatively, "if you are, as I suppose, Nereids, I thought you were sisters. I never read about a brother."

"We are fifty sisters, in fact," replied Miss Hetty. "Our brother is never mentioned in the stories. He is, perhaps, not a brother exactly. We are not to ask, but he was raised as a brother and is half of the sea and half of the land."

"A brother is what I am," chuckled the pale gentleman, "and the only thing I want is my pipes." Striding to the table, he quickly took them up and pocketed them.

A week later Aunt Nasturtium brought a tuna casserole for dinner. When they had finished eating, she repeated the story as the twins had told it to her, which was with numerous omissions. She repeated it triumphantly as a lesson well learned.

"The brother returned abruptly and asked you to bring a lawyer and witnesses to the house. He said the sisters could not leave unless you did this. So you did. He paid the lawyer to make out a deed giving the house and all its contents to you two. After the lawyer left, there was a great thunderstorm. The ladies kissed you good-bye and left, in the rain. And the brother? He left, too." She chuckled complacently. "Well, well, wages *and* a house full of books and antiques. So that's why you stuck it out, and were so sweet to those old ladies. You two *are* clever, far cleverer than I thought. Well done!"

Jane shuddered. Aunt Nasturtium's praise was worse than her blame. Daddy looked pained. John sat stonily silent, sketching away. Jane glanced at him. John tilted the pad slightly so that she could see. The page was dense with fauns, satyrs, and centaurs, all playing pipes. From ocean waves and foam rose shells and Nereids with the faces of young girls, and with the faces of old women; one face was weeping.

"Can you play that song again?" he whispered.

Reversible

by Octavio Paz

*Look at the lines in this poem, which
appears in Spanish on the next page. Why
do you think the poet arranged the lines
this way? Does the poem bring to mind
any parts of* A Wrinkle in Time?

In space
            I am
inside of me
            the space
5   outside of me
                  the space
nowhere
            I am
outside of me
10   in space
inside
        is space
outside of it
            nowhere
15   I am
        in space
etcetera

En el espacio
                estoy
dentro de mí
                el espacio
5   fuera de mí
                el espacio
en ningún lado
                        estoy
fuera de mí
10   en el espacio
dentro
        está el espacio
fuera de sí
                en ningún lado
15   estoy
        en el espacio
etcétera

Behind Bars

by Fadwa Tuqan

*Sadly, this poet may have written "Behind Bars"
from her direct experience. Most people have
not been arrested. What can we learn from a
Palestinian poet writing about an experience
that most of us will never have?*

My mother's phantom hovers here
her forehead shines before my eyes
like the light of stars
She might be thinking of me now,
5   dreaming

        (Before my arrest
        I drew letters in a book
        new and old
        I painted roses
10   grown with blood
        and my mother was near me
        blessing my painting)

I see her
on her face silence and loneliness now
15   and in the house
silence and loneliness
My satchel there on the bookshelf
and my school uniform
on the hanger
20   I see her hand reaching out
brushing the dust from it
I follow my mother's steps
and listen to her thoughts
yearning for her arms and the face of day

from World of the Brain

by Alvin and Virginia Silverstein

The brain is a complex organ long studied by scientists. We've learned a lot about states of mind, yet many mysteries remain. Does this information help you appreciate the awesome power of IT?

It is possible to induce a trance state in other people by the technique of *hypnosis*. A hypnotized person may seem to be asleep, but actually the brain waves are those of someone who is alert and awake. Hypnosis permits a person to relax and focus attention very narrowly. This state differs from biofeedback in that the attention is focused outward rather than inward, and the person plays a passive role, obeying the orders of the hypnotist. It is a common but inaccurate belief that only stupid or gullible people can be hypnotized; actually, going into a hypnotic trance requires a fine degree of concentration. Under hypnosis a person may be able to perform feats of strength that would be impossible under normal conditions. The mind can be guided to reduce its awareness of pain to such a degree that surgical operations can be performed without anesthesia. It has been reported that hypnosis can be used to stop bleeding and even to cure some kinds of diseases. Warts, small unruly skin growths, are caused by a virus infection, but they respond very well to hypnosis, disappearing as though by magic under the power of the hypnotist's suggestion.

Probably you have seen demonstrations of hypnosis presented as entertainment on the stage or on television, but the techniques are used also for medical purposes by qualified doctors. Police sometimes use hypnosis to aid in their investigations. The theory is that the greater concentration of a person under hypnosis makes it possible to remember vivid details that cannot be called up in the conscious state. To some degree this is true. In times of stress, such as during a crime, the body is flooded with the hormones epinephrine (adrenaline) and norepinephrine (noradrenaline). There is evidence that norepinephrine, acting as a neurotransmitter in the brain, can work as a "print" instruction, helping to fix memories in vivid detail. But memories formed under great stress may be difficult to recall, because calling them up into the conscious mind also calls up feelings of pain and fear, and the brain defensively suppresses them. Hypnosis helps a person to recall the memories while damping down awareness of the painful emotions that went with them. There is a problem with the recollection of events under hypnosis, however. People in a hypnotic state are extremely suggestible, and the wording of the questions may—deliberately or inadvertently—cause the mind to change remembered details or even invent memories of things that did not happen. For this reason the courts are usually very cautious about accepting testimony obtained under hypnosis, and the use of hypnosis in the investigation of a crime may even discredit the witness's later testimony, given in the conscious state.

Since before the beginning of recorded history, there have been people who claimed to be able to do things that were beyond the powers of the ordinary senses. There have been claims of *telepathy* (reading other people's minds), *clairvoyance* (knowing what is happening somewhere else without any communication by normal means), and *psychokinesis* (causing physical objects to move by mental powers; for example, influencing dice to fall in certain ways or bending a metal rod). People have claimed to be able to find water by *dowsing* with a forked stick, and others have claimed to diagnose or heal ailments by mental powers or to communicate with spirits of the dead.

Usually investigations have revealed some natural explanation, or even a deliberate hoax, but a small number of cases remain that have not yet been explained satisfactorily. Unexplainable feats of these types fall into the category known as *extrasensory perception (ESP)*.

Most scientists have mixed feelings about ESP. They may concede that there may be something there, but many have the feeling that the subject is not quite respectable. Some serious investigations have been made. A favorite technique is to have the volunteer guess the pictures on cards either held or looked at by another volunteer or by the investigator. A special deck of cards is commonly used, consisting of five each of five picture cards: a cross, a circle, a star, wavy lines, and a square. The cards are shuffled so that they come up in random order. Merely guessing would give an average score of five correct of the twenty-five total answers. Scores much higher than five would be an indication of some kind of ESP operating, and some of the experiments have yielded statistically significant results, even when the volunteer and the investigator are separated by a distance of miles. But ESP ability, if it does exist, is a touchy thing. It does not always work; the results are not regularly repeatable, not even with the same person under the same conditions. This is what makes scientists so uncomfortable about ESP. Normally, they depend on being able to repeat the work of other scientists and get the same results.

It is difficult to speculate how ESP phenomena could work; if they do exist, there are obviously some laws of nature that science has not yet discovered. If the secrets of ESP are ever discovered, it seems fairly certain that they will be found to lie in the human brain.

from It's Our World, Too!

by Phillip Hoose

You never know when people will fight back. Andrew Holleman was only 12 when he decided to resist, just as the characters in A Wrinkle in Time *did. What does he demonstrate about taking a stand and accepting responsibility for the care of the earth?*

One afternoon in late August, Andrew Holleman's mother stood at the table reading a letter that had just come in the mail. She seemed upset. "What is it, Mom?" he asked. Shaking her head, she passed it to Andrew.

Andrew's eyes narrowed. It was from a company whose president was announcing that he wanted to develop the private land next to Andrew's yard. The developer wanted to build 180 condominium units.

Andrew was stunned. He had loved and studied and explored that land ever since he could remember. Each summer, he pulled bass from the stream that ran through it. Every winter, he played hockey on the frozen stream with his friends. Using their field guides, he and a friend had learned to identify nearly all the plants and animals that lived there. Andrew especially liked to follow the stream back to a flat rock, where he would sit, whittling and thinking. From that rock he had seen deer and foxes pass by. Once a red-tailed hawk had settled onto a snag about ten feet away and stared at him, cocking its head as if it were trying to figure out what sort of creature Andrew was. The thought of losing all that was unbearable.

Andrew looked at the letter's final sentence. His parents were invited to an open meeting at town hall to hear the developer describe his plans. The meeting was only four weeks away. Sitting at his kitchen table, Andrew went through a kind of metamorphosis. His initial shock melted into anger, and then the anger changed into a cold determination. Somehow Andrew Holleman was going to stop that development.

"Are You Still Looking?"

Andrew needed information, fast. He knew there were laws in Massachusetts, where he lived, that said when you could and couldn't put buildings on wetlands. And most of the land next door was wet all the time.

His mother dropped him off at the library, and soon Andrew was staring at bookcases full of Massachusetts law books. He needed to find the Hatch Act, which his parents had told him was the law that controlled the development of wetlands in Massachusetts.

Two hours later, Andrew's mother returned to find him barely visible behind a mountain of law books. She picked out a book of her own and sat down. A few minutes later, she heard him shout. Several nearby readers looked up. "Finally I found it," Andrew remembers. "It was clear: The Hatch Act said it was illegal to build within one hundred feet of a wetland unless you had a permit.

"I asked the librarian what else I should read. She reached behind her desk and handed me the master plan for my town, Chelmsford." A master plan is a guide to the way all the land in a town can be used.

It tells which land can be developed for industry, which land can support houses or apartments, and which must be left open for parks or nature areas.

Quickly he found the land by his house on a map that came with the plan. "I could see that the developer wanted to develop 16.3 acres; that's how big the site was. But 8.5 acres were zoned as wetlands and 5.6 of the rest were considered to be poor soil. It looked like only 2.2 acres were considered developable."

Weary but happy, Andrew got up from his desk and pulled on his jacket. Now he had the ammunition he needed.

"Please Sign the Attached Sheet."

Andrew knew the developer's plan was probably illegal, but that didn't mean anyone else knew, or that anyone else would care. He needed a way to educate people about the developer's plan and its weaknesses before the meeting.

He decided to write a petition opposing the development and ask the registered voters who lived in the neighborhood to sign it. He could then send copies to local politicians. If they could see that most voters were against the development, Andrew reasoned, they might be persuaded.

The petition had to be short and to the point. "I knew it couldn't be more than a page long, because people tend to ignore longer things," he says. "I gave basic information about the site and the law. Then I said, 'If you agree with me that this land shouldn't be developed, please sign the attached sheet.'"

Every night for the next few weeks, Andrew raced home from school, did his homework, bolted down dinner, and then headed out to gather signatures. He was very patient. "Some nights I would be out for two hours and I'd get only five signatures, because people would bring me into their house and offer me cookies while they discussed it with me. That was fine with me. I didn't want to get in a hurry and leave out information. I wanted to make sure I had a chance to answer every question they could think of."

Andrew also created a petition at school. Even though they couldn't vote, he hoped his schoolmates would want to add their voices to the fight. "Some kids didn't agree with me, but the majority did. I just kept on going."

And he continued his research. He called the state Audubon Society's Environmental Health Line and asked for ideas. Dr. Dorothy Arvison, a staff biologist, told him how to get a list of the state's endangered and threatened species from the Massachusetts Division of Fisheries and Wildlife.

When the list arrived in the mail, Andrew recognized three species—the wood turtle, the yellow salamander, and the great blue heron—that lived on his land. He remembered that one day he had found a wood turtle shell in an old trap. He had picked it up and taken it back to his room. The list gave him an idea for how that old shell could be useful. He thought the turtle would approve.

Organizing an Ambush

As the night of the meeting approached, Andrew went over his list of things to do. A neighbor had already contacted some reporters, who had said they'd be there. Andrew had written letters to newspaper editors opposing the development. The petition now had over 180 signatures, and there was no one left to visit. He had sent copies to town officials and to his state senators and representatives.

Finally he wrote a speech to give at the meeting. Every night after his homework, Andrew gathered his parents, his brother, and sister and asked them to help him rehearse.

He opened by saying how much he loved the land. He said it provided a home for three endangered species. He said that the sewage from so much development would poison the local groundwater— and Chelmsford's wells, the town's drinking water. He even proposed an alternative site for development: the old drive-in theater. Raising the wood turtle's shell aloft and shaking it at his family, Andrew ended by listing all the reasons why the developer's proposal should be rejected. "Well?" Andrew would ask his family, totally inspired. "What do you think?" "Speak more slowly," his brother would suggest. "How about doing it one more time?" his mother would add.

When it came time to leave for the meeting, Andrew felt the calmness and confidence that comes with having prepared carefully. He had been organizing almost nonstop for a month. The trap was set, and Andrew was ready.

"Where Did All These People Come From?"

At 7:30, the developer and town officials watched in amazement as hundreds of Chelmsford residents lined up outside the town hall. The developer had sent letters to only fifty nearby residents. Where had all these people come from? And where were they going to put them all? First they changed rooms to the selectmen's office but even then the crowd spilled out into the hall. Finally a town official begged the girls' high school basketball coach to end practice early and let them have the gym. By 8:00, there were over 250 people in the bleachers.

The developer began by presenting his plan and then asked if anyone wanted to speak. Andrew rose and walked slowly to the front of the room, carrying his note cards and the turtle shell. There was applause, and then quiet.

Andrew's speech went perfectly. The only surprise came when Andrew suggested the developer build instead at the site of the old drive-in movie theater. "I found out the guy had already started a condominium there."

The struggle was far from over. Although now it was clear that most neighbors opposed the development, the developer wasn't about to give up. Over the next ten months, he presented his plans to the conservation commission, zoning board, appeals board, and selectmen. They all had to say yes for his plan to go through. Andrew was determined to help them say no.

"I went to every meeting, usually with my parents," Andrew remembers. "Sometimes I went to two or three meetings a week. Usually they were on school nights, and often I didn't get home until eleven. My mother kept saying, 'Don't get burned out; if you need to stop now, it's okay—you've already made a good try.'"

Because they were together so much, Andrew came to know the developer. Although he hated the man's plan, he didn't hate the man himself. "It's like how lawyers can be fighting tooth and nail in a courtroom one minute and then be friendly out in the hall," Andrew says. "That's the way we were. When it was time for business, we got down to business."

The developer seemed to respect Andrew as a worthy opponent, even if he was young—although once, in a meeting, he hollered, "I'm not going to discuss hydrogeological information with a twelve-year-old!" "He was really worked up," Andrew recalls. "I didn't take it personally."

Together with a few neighbors, Andrew's parents formed a neighborhood association and went door-to-door asking for money to hire a lawyer and a scientist to testify at hearings. They ended up raising $16,000.

Dr. Arvidson, the Audubon biologist, never seemed to run out of ideas for Andrew. Once, while she was giving him a long list of suggestions, Andrew interrupted. "Hey, I'm only twelve years old," he told her. "That's no excuse," she said, and went right on talking.

Victory!

Finally it came time to test whether the soil at the site could hold the enormous amount of sewage—dishwater, bath water, toilet water, water from washing machines—that would be created in 180 condominiums.

While Andrew, his father, and several town officials watched, the developer fired up a backhoe and dug about fifteen deep holes in the soil. Muddy water quickly filled all the holes but two and then spilled out onto the grass. That meant sewage from the proposed condominiums would flow right down into drinking water. The plan had failed the test.

Two weeks later, the zoning board of appeals met

to make a final decision. The developer, sensing that he was about to lose, asked to withdraw his application. That way he would be able to try again, for fewer condominiums. But the board ruled that the site was simply not suitable for development. Andrew had won!

When the zoning board gave its ruling, Andrew felt like shattering the hearing room with a mighty whoop, but instead, he walked over and shook the developer's hand. No reason to burn bridges, he told himself.

Now Andrew is hard at work with his ultimate plan, which is to convince the town to buy the land and use it as a nature preserve. He won't rest until the land he loves is absolutely safe. "If I don't do it," he says, "no one else is going to."

The Dark Princess

by Richard Kennedy

How were the children able to overcome IT? Read this modern fairy tale to find out if a similar power is at work.

There was a child born who was so beautiful that no one could look at her without blinking, and she was a Princess. Each day and each year she became more beautiful. When she was ten, those who spoke to her looked over her shoulder, or turned their heads while speaking. It was as if a great light shone out of her face. When she was a young lady and ready to marry, no one could look into her face at all. The sight would strike them blind. And another thing. The Princess herself was totally blind.

She was not born blind, but became blind year by year as she became more beautiful. The Royal Physician explained the matter to her parents, the King and Queen. He said the condition was caused by a "frontal optical reversal of the cognitive processes acting on the stereoscopic image-blending phenomenon which resulted in a transposed focal plane bilaterally projecting her sight into a dark area of her brain." He could put it more simply than this. "It is like a dark cloud that blocks out the sun. It could pass at any time."

And so, since it could pass at any time, the King and Queen kept her blindness a secret. That was easy enough to do, since it was impossible for anyone to look at the Princess directly, and a great, long-haired dog led her way and guarded her step, and she had the measure of every chair and table in the palace, and every bush and tree in the Royal Garden. Her ear was so clever that she knew the footstep of everyone on tile or on carpet, and their voices, of course. From the rustle of their clothes, she knew what others were wearing, and from the tinkle of metal and the clink of stone, their ornaments and jewelry, and no one could sit so quietly in a room that she would not know he was there.

One day, when the Princess was walking in the garden, the King made a wonderful discovery. He was standing at a stained-glass window inside the palace as she passed, and his discovery was that he could look into her face through the dark glass and not be blinded. He called her and spoke to her face-to-face through the window and was awed by her beauty.

Everyone in the Kingdom who could afford it got himself a piece of colored glass to behold the Princess, and watched her come and go with her dog, her head held in a slight attentive cock, as if she were listening to music they could not hear, or pursuing some fancy in her mind. She carried herself with such aloofness that some thought she was conceited about her great beauty and could not bother to take notice of anyone else. Some said it was only modesty and a sign of good upbringing. But it was neither. She was merely counting her steps and listening to the many sounds that tell the way in total darkness, and feeling the trembling of the leash she held as the dog informed her of a chair or table out of place, a new-dug hole in the garden, a limb across a path, or anything else amiss or strange in her way. The people did not suspect she was blind.

Now this was the state of affairs when the first Prince came to the Kingdom to consider the girl for a bride, and through his glass—yes, even so darkly—

she was as beautiful to him as anyone he had ever seen, and he loved her at once. After a while of courtly good manners, they walked in the garden alone, led by the Princess's dog. They stopped by a flowering bush, and the Prince looked at her through his glass and spoke.

"Forgive me," he said, "but this past hour has been an age to me, and there would be nothing left of me but dust if I would wait through a season of wooing to declare myself to you. Let me be plain and quick while I am not yet faded to a shadow by the sight of you. You are more beautiful than anyone I have ever seen or could imagine, and I am helplessly in love with you already."

"Are you?" said the Princess, touching a blossom.

"Forsooth," said the Prince, "my very self with love has leaped from me. I have forgotten who I am, in love. I would not know my face in a mirror. Marry me. Come with me and be my Queen, or say no to me and tell me my name so I may despair over the sound of it forever."

The Princess had been told that the Prince was handsome and well set up, and she had no reason to doubt it. His speech was fair (though a bit extravagant), his manners pleasant, and his voice sounded sweet to her.

"If you love me," said the Princess, "then you may prove it to me."

The Prince dropped to one knee. "Only tell me how," he said. "Any vow, any venture, any danger, any dare . . ."

"Look at me," said the Princess.

"What?"

"Take away your piece of colored glass and look at me directly."

"But . . . but . . ." the Prince stammered, getting to

his feet again. "They say that, that if one does . . ."

"Yes," said the Princess, "if you do, you will be blinded."

"But to be *blind!*" said the Prince. "How awful. Certainly you wouldn't want me to be blind! Sight is more valuable than anything but life itself. How could you love me then?"

"Only then *could* I love you. Then I would believe that you truly loved me, and I would love you."

The Prince protested such an outrageous test of his love, and drew upon arguments from philosophy, law, physics, chemistry, and astronomy to declare the reasons why he could not meet the test. "Give me another test," he demanded.

"There is no other," said the Princess, and plucking a blossom she turned and walked back to the palace.

The Prince rode away that same day, and the King came to the Princess in her rooms and said, "Did the Prince not please you?"

"He pleased me well enough," she said, brushing the dog with long sweeping strokes, "and I might have loved him."

"But then why did he leave?" asked the King.

"Because he could not love *me,* Father."

"Ye gods, he must have been blind! Excuse me, dear."

"No, he was not blind," said the Princess. "He would have hated that."

And so for a year the princes came, and each in his manner, shy or bold, plain or poetic, declared he had lost his heart in love for the Princess. But none would lose his sight for it, and all of them went away in a silent and puzzled wonder.

Likewise were the King and Queen puzzled. Princes were now coming from very far away, and soon there would be none left at all to come. They wondered—had the princes suspected that the girl was blind? The King and Queen had chosen to keep this a secret, and did not consider it so very unfair since the girl was likely to regain her sight at any moment. And besides, her blindness was a small thing in comparison to her beauty. They simply could not understand. Of course, they did not know of the test the girl proposed. And none could pass that test.

The Princess by this time had satisfied herself that she would not marry, and in these later days she became sad. It was not so much that she was sad because she would not have a husband, for those who do not marry can be happy, but her sadness was in her doubt that there was such a thing as love in the world. So many had told her that they loved her, but none of them would prove it in the way she asked. Then what was this love they spoke about? She was tired of the word.

The Princess walked more slowly than usual now, and sometimes she sat by a window for hours without moving, and she took no delight in stories or music, and if dessert had not been served after supper, she would not have noticed. It is a bad sadness to believe that there is no love in the world, and people have hanged themselves for less gloomy discoveries.

But it was worse yet than that. Believing that there was no love in the world was her lesser sorrow. Her greater sorrow was this: What if a Prince *should* give up his eyesight out of love for her? What had she to give in return? She was already blind. Just one time there was a Prince who had paused thoughtfully when she told him the test, and for a terrible few throbbing moments she feared that this one would actually go blind for her, and a strange agony rose in her breast, and she was relieved when the Prince began his protest.

Later and alone, the poor girl concluded that her fear and agony in those moments was for the reason that even though there may be love in the world, there was no love in herself. She had nothing to give to prove it. That was her greater sorrow. She believed she could not love.

When her thoughts followed along these dismal lines for too long a time, and she found herself wondering how it would feel to fall from the great tower, and how long it would take before she was broken on the ground, the Princess shook her head and hurried to the kitchen to have a picnic packed for herself, and she took herself away from her thoughts of oblivion, out through the garden and beyond the great stone lion gates on the path that went down to the ocean. Her dog led the way, and as the surf grew louder in the distance and the first smell of salt air came to her, she hummed a tune to raise her spirits. Only the sea was large enough to fill the emptiness she sometimes felt inside herself, and there at the edge of the land where a cliff dropped into the crashing surf below, she would eat her picnic lunch and drink a glass of wine, and sometimes she would smile.

On this day there was someone else out on a picnic at that place. The Court Fool was sitting with his legs dangling over the side of the cliff, and next to him was a bottle of wine and some chicken bones. The dog barked, and the Fool turned to look. He blinked, and quickly got out his piece of colored glass and watched the Princess approach. As usual, she seemed to take no notice of him at all, and it was not his place to greet her first. What a strange, distracted girl she seemed to be, and he concluded that she was probably caught up in a daydream. In fact, she came walking out onto the cliff so purposefully and yet so much like a sleepwalker, that he was certain she was going to walk right over the edge, and he called, "Look out!"

Hardly were the words out of his mouth when she stopped.

"Look out?" she said, turning toward him but looking over his head. "Look out for what? I am exactly five steps from the edge of the cliff." She had recognized his voice, of course. "What are you doing out here, Fool?"

"Well, as you see, Princess, I came for a little picnic like yourself. Roast chicken, a little wine. Will the dog eat the bones?"

"You are certainly a fool if you don't know that chicken bones are dangerous for dogs," she said, and she spread out a cloth to set her picnic basket on. The Fool raked the bones over the side and watched them fall into the surf below. He looked at the Princess again through his colored glass, then took a drink of his wine. He had never been so close to her before, and certainly he had never been alone with her. What could he say? He ventured a common subject: "They say another Prince is coming to visit next week, from very far away."

"I have heard that," said the Princess, breaking some bread and putting a piece of cheese in her mouth. "It matters little."

The Fool had intended to follow up on such a conversation, for he was safe and in his place to talk of the visiting princes, their fine dress and horses, and to gossip of neighboring kingdoms, but instead he said, "Why don't you ever laugh at me?"

The Princess stopped chewing. She started to make a stern face at the Fool, but then she shrugged. "I do laugh, now and again." The truth was, of course, that she had never been able to see his funny antics when he entertained at court, and remembered to laugh only sometimes, when the others laughed.

"No you don't laugh, not really," said the Fool, "and I am a student of laughing. No, you don't laugh, not like the others. And the others laugh when I see them about the hallways and do a face and a little step for them, but you seem to ignore me."

The Princess folded some ham into her bread. "Perhaps you are not such a funny fool as you think you are."

The Fool plucked at the grass and sprinkled it into the wind blowing up past his legs. "I would think my face was funny enough," he said, and they sat and listened to the ocean. "But I *can* make you laugh," said the Fool at last. "Yes, I could make you laugh this very moment if I wanted to."

"I guarantee you cannot," said the Princess, and she smiled. "Stand on your head, stretch out your cheeks and ears, look at me under your legs, and squash your nose. You couldn't make me laugh."

"Then I will, just to show you," said the Fool. "And I will do it with words alone. Be ready to laugh, now, for here it is that will amuse you greatly, and only three words will do it." He took a double gulp of wine and then said, "I love you."

The Princess did not laugh. She lowered her head and gazed very solemnly toward the ground. Presently she said, "Yes, for a Fool to love a Princess—I suppose that might be funny. However, since it isn't true, it isn't funny. Two-score princes have come and gone, and all of them said that they loved me. But none of them did, and you do not, either."

The Princess poured herself a glass of wine and took a sip. "There is no such thing as love, and that's why I don't laugh at you now, and why I rarely laugh. What you think you love you do not, really. I am only beautiful, and if you lost the way to see me, you would not love me."

"No," he said. "It is not your beauty I love, it is *you* I love, it is your *ways* I love. A Fool may look closely to know who a person is, and with little insult, for he need only wag his nose to be excused. And though I have seen you only darkly, I have seen you deeply, and it is you yourself that I love."

Now the Princess did laugh. "Let me tell you something. Will you promise to keep it a secret?"

"In my heart," said the Fool. And so the Princess told him why she had not chosen a Prince to marry, and how she had put her test to them, and how they all had declined to look at her directly and go blind for their love.

"I would be blind for you," said the Fool.

The Princess gathered up her things and put them in the basket. "Then you would be a fool for sure." She folded her picnic cloth and stood up. "Yes, you would be the best fool of all. Any of the princes would have had me for a bride upon looking at me directly. But I cannot marry you, and you would have nothing for it but darkness."

The Fool smiled to himself and nodded. Then he too stood up next to her and looked at her through his colored glass. The Princess could feel the Fool's sadness, and she spoke again before turning to leave.

"You are a good and fortunate fool to believe in love, but your sadness is not as great as it could be. Mine is greater. Remember, I do not believe in love."

"But you *must* believe in love," said the Fool. "I would go blind that you do, for that alone I would go blind."

And then the Princess was reminded of her greater

sorrow—her sorrow that even though another might one day give his sight out of love for her, she had nothing to give in return. She shook her head.

"Ah, dear Fool, we could be certain of nothing except that you would be blind. How could I believe? I have nothing to give in return. But here, let me touch your hand before I go."

The Princess reached out her hand, and she felt a thin, smooth object placed in her palm. She caught her breath to cry out, but the Fool cried, "Oh, oh . . ." and she heard him stumble backwards, and heard his foot slide on the cliff's edge. He fell without a sound, and she heard him splash in the surf below. She dropped the picnic basket and the piece of colored glass, touched her toe to the edge of the cliff, and leaped into the water to save him, for he was only newly blind.

And there in the darkness below they touched for a moment, and then they drowned.

And in that moment they touched, the sun rose a million times for them, and the Princess and the Fool could see each other and all the things of life and the world more clearly than but a dozen people since the beginning of time. And that moment they touched outlasted the life of the King and Queen, and outlasted the life of the Kingdom. And that moment they touched is lasting still, and will outlast us, too.

The Sparrow

by Ivan Turgenev

*In this sketch the author shows a
sympathy for the weak that is reflected in
much of his work. Can Turgenev's
reflections on the sparrow give you insight
into Meg, Calvin, and Charles Wallace?*

I was returning from a day's hunting and was
walking toward the house along an alley in my
garden. My dog was running ahead of me.

Suddenly she slowed her pace and began to
advance stealthily, as though she had caught scent of
game.

I looked down the path and saw a young sparrow
with a streak of yellow near its beak and a bit of puff
on its head. It had fallen out of the nest. (A strong
wind was swaying the birch trees.) The tiny bird sat
there trying helplessly to use its barely grown wings.

My dog was stealing up to the infant sparrow
when, abruptly, an old black-chested bird fell like a
stone right in front of the dog's face, and with all its
feathers standing on end, misshapen, uttering a
desperate and pitiful chirp, it hopped once and then
again in the direction of the dog's open jaw.

The bird had thrown itself in front of the dog to
shield its young one, but its own small body was
trembling with terror, its little voice was frenzied and
hoarse, and it was numb with fright—it was
sacrificing itself!

What a huge monster the dog must have seemed to
the mother sparrow! Nevertheless, it could not bear
to stay on its high, safe perch in the tree. A force

stronger than its will to remain alive made it hurl itself to the rescue.

My Treasure, the dog, stopped still and then backed up. Evidently she, too, recognized that force. . . .

I hastened to call off the puzzled dog and went on my way, awed.

Yes, do not laugh. I was awed by that small, heroic bird—by its impulse of love.

Love, I felt more than ever, is stronger than death and the fear of death. Only through love is life sustained and nourished.

Colony

by Rick Wernli

*What if IT had triumphed? Could the
result have been anything like the
situation in "The Colony"? As you read,
notice that the story is divided into thirds:
"Year One," "Year One Hundred," and
"Year One Thousand." What happens
during this span of time? What is about to
happen at the end of the story?*

YEAR ONE

It was raining in Omaha.

Beyond the schoolroom window, the world was
lost in a haze of gray shadows and darkness, a scene
blurred and twisted by the rippling streaks of water
that danced outside the glass. The droplets tapped
incessantly against the pane, like something invisible
seeking a way inside.

Mathew adjusted his glasses and turned to face the
class. The children had gathered their chairs in a
circle near the bookshelf, as they did every morning,
and one of the girls was entertaining the group with
a very impromptu rain dance. He smiled and checked
his watch . . . let her dance.

As he closed the door he glanced into the hall and
saw a yellow slicker peeking around the stairwell
corner. He looked back at the other children and
then walked across the corridor.

Sitting at the top of the stairs was a small boy with
dark hair, his slicker still wet, the hood pulled back,

the buttons undone. The teacher was surprised to find him crying.

"Hey, little buddy, what's wrong?" He sat next to the boy. "Want to tell me about it?"

The child tried to speak, but the words were only sobs, broken and meaningless.

"Take it easy." Mathew put his hand on the boy's shoulder. "It's okay."

Little arms clutched his waist, and the small face buried itself in his shoulder.

"Momma." The voice was weak. "They took my momma."

Another one?

Slowly his arms encircled the child, and his lips formed useless words.

"It's all right. I understand. Don't cry."

The boy sniffled and sighed, then grew quiet, but the tears went on flowing, soaking into the man's jacket.

"I'm sure your mother will be fine."

The child shook his head.

"Sure she will. They probably just want to ask her some questions or something."

"No . . . I heard Grandma on the phone. 'They'll kill her,' that's what she said. "They'll kill her for writing that book.'"

"Maybe you didn't hear it right."

"She said they'd kill Momma, just like Poppa, 'cause she wrote bad stories."

"Your mother wrote about Colonists?" He almost knew without asking.

The boy nodded. "She hates them, more than Poppa did. She says they're monsters."

"There are no monsters."

The boy looked up, his eyes red. "Grandma says they're monsters, too."

"Colonists aren't monsters. They just aren't like us, that's all."

"But . . . are you sure?"

The teacher forced a smile. "Sure I'm sure. In fact, that's what we'll be talking about in class this morning. I have an idea. Why don't you sit next to me and be my assistant today. Would you like that?"

"Don't know." The boy shrugged. "Guess so."

"Good. Let's not keep everybody waiting, okay? We'll talk more later."

"Okay."

The boy set his rain gear aside at the door and then joined the other children in the circle of chairs.

"Who knows what day it is?" Mathew prompted.

"April!" someone shouted, and the others laughed.

"April is close. It's Friday, April tenth, and that means one year ago the Colonists came to Earth. Who can tell us how they got here?"

"The spaceship!" several children yelled at once.

"That's right, a big, gray spaceship, shaped like . . . ?"

"An egg!"

"Right. And where is this spaceship?"

"New York City!"

"Good. And what's it doing there?"

Blank faces.

"You're right. It's not really doing anything, is it? It's just floating in the air over the United Nations Building. Who knows where the spaceship came from?"

Again, silence.

"Right. Nobody knows where the Colonists come from, because they haven't told us yet. There's an awful lot about these space travelers we just don't understand, but we're learning all the time, and today I want to tell you about some of the really interesting things we do know."

The teacher turned to the boy at his side. "Mister Assistant, would you show us where China is?"

The child hurried from his seat to stand before the wall map, pointing to a large, red splotch.

"Very good."

Wearing a fragile smile, the boy resumed his seat.

"China is very far away from here. That's where the Colonists decided to make their home on our planet. They call it 'Colony,' and it's made of domes, lots of domes all connected, like a big bunch of bubbles. They live inside these bubbles, because they can't breathe regular air like we do."

There were noises outside the window, vague motions beyond the glass, traffic, activity, voices.

"Uh, the air they need to breathe is called 'methane,' and they fill up those bubbles with it."

The noise came closer, moving up the stairway and into the hall—footsteps, movement, angry protests.

"The Colonists are very different from us. . . ."

The sound of a scuffle came from beyond the door.

"I'll just go see what's happening outside," he said, but he was barely out of his seat when the door suddenly swung open.

Across the threshold strode a woman in gray uniform with a United Nations emblem at the lapel. She wore a Colonial radiocom on her belt and a holstered automatic at her side. Behind her, men and women were leading children from other classrooms toward the stairs as several uniformed guards stood watch.

The teacher just stood there, staring.

"My name is Captain Ryan," the woman told him. "I have orders from the secretary general to evacuate the premises. You will escort your class down to the bus lines in an orderly fashion, beginning immediately."

"I will not! What is all this!? I was never informed . . ."

"No one was informed, sir. I have my orders."

"To hell with your orders! Where's the principal?"

"She's receiving medical attention at the moment. I would advise you not to interfere." The woman unsnapped the holster with gloved fingers. "Clear?"

"You can't do this!"

"I have a Colonial directive that says otherwise, and that's all the authority I need. Now lead these children downstairs."

"No . . ." Mathew swallowed nervously. "I refuse."

"Very well."

Two men in uniform entered at the captain's signal.

"All right, children." She smiled. "We're all going on a nice bus ride."

The men moved among the students, herding them toward the door, and the children were too frightened to resist.

"Where are you taking them?"

"Manhattan," the woman replied. "Special housing has been provided . . ."

"New York! But the parents—"

"Parental consent is not required."

The uniformed men paused at the door to let the children don their rain gear.

"What's this all about? Why are you doing this?"

"You'll get your evacuation instructions on the broadcast networks tonight," the Captain replied. "This area's been selected as the next site for Colony construction. Everything within twenty miles of here—"

"Next site!? What are you talking about?"

"The secretary was informed last night. More Colonists are coming. The seedship was just the beginning. Colony will be expanded."

"But . . . I don't understand what this has to do with the children!"

"It's for their own good," the woman assured him. "They'll be just fine. Better off, in fact."

"What do you mean?"

"It's not something I'm at liberty to discuss."

"Gene fixing! That's it, isn't it? I've heard stories—"

"You shouldn't listen to idle talk."

"But they're just children!"

"The technique only works on children. Don't be so concerned. We're extending their lives."

Suddenly the boy in the yellow slicker ran from the line and threw his arms around the teacher.

"Don't let them take me!" he cried. "Please!"

They both struggled to hold on as men in gray uniforms pried them apart, one wrapping Mathew in a headlock as the other dragged the child, kicking and screaming, from the room.

"Please!" the boy yelled, and then he was gone.

The teacher stumbled forward as the arm around his throat released him, and his glasses fell to the floor. He moved quickly for the door, but the captain's drawn revolver stopped him.

"Don't."

He could only stand by and watch as the last few children were taken from the room.

"Be sensible," the woman said, holstering her weapon. "There's nothing you can do. There's nothing anyone can do."

"We could try."

She shook her head, then turned and started for the door.

"I was wrong," Mathew said softly.

"What?"

"They are monsters." His eyes were dark and cold. "And so are we."

YEAR ONE HUNDRED

There was a parade.

High on the rooftops, the children looked up in wonder, as many had a century before, but it was not the great seedship that held their interest on this day. Featureless, motionless, the huge gray ovoid hung effortlessly above the city, just as it had for one hundred years. It was now too commonplace to be an object of curiosity, even for children.

It was the parade they awaited. Public ceremonies were always amusing, and this promised to be an event without parallel. "Be part of the greatest celebration in history!" declared the broadcast networks. "The Great Centennial of Colony Earth is upon us! Be happy!" So the children were ready. A parade, after all, was a good reason to party.

At the center of the main group, a small boy with long, dark hair moved slowly from child to child selling small tabs of micro, each shaped like a smooth, gray egg. He slid gracefully across the rooftop on silent airskates, pausing once to drink from an offered flask of brandywine, then moving on to distribute his wares. Between sales, he occasionally glanced up at the oncoming parade.

Amid the distant sound of music and cheering crowds, thousands of wind-borne vessels approached in wide formation. Floats and flyers and balloons of every description filled the horizon, all trailing banners and plumes of colored smoke. Kites and gliders circled the smaller floats, rising and swooping in daring patterns to excite and amaze, while the large balloons carried tails of prismwire to dazzle the eye.

Reaching the fringe of the group, the boy paused before turning back, surprised to find a girl sitting alone at the roof's edge, her feet dangling over the precipice. She showed no interest in the parade, her eyes downcast. He considered her a moment, wary of her mood, then shrugged and smiled. "Why not?"

She looked up as he drew nearer, then turned away, pretending not to notice him.

"Day." He smiled, sitting beside her.

"Day," she replied, still looking away.

"Can't see the parade too well from here." He strained his neck to gaze over the heads of children standing behind them.

"Hadn't noticed." The girl frowned.

"See real good over there," he noted, pointing to the front of the group.

"So, go over there," she said, and her eyes turned their pain and anger at him.

"Intend to, don't worry. Just thought you might need chemistry."

She stared at the small gray pill in his outstretched hand, then shook her head. "Not today."

"Why not?" the boy asked, gesturing toward the parade with a sweep of his arm. "New Year's Day, right?"

The children nearby began to cheer as the music grew louder. It was Colony music, but performed live by humans with real Earth instruments. The parade was getting close.

"Good reason to party," he reminded her, hoping to raise her spirits. "Hundred-year anniversary, know?"

"Really been a hundred years?" She sighed. Her eyes were damp as she glanced up at the Colony ship overhead. "That long?"

Confused, but sympathetic, the boy followed her gaze.

"Should be happy," he said softly. "Should be grateful. Nobody gets sick. Nobody grows old. Nobody goes hungry. Hundred years of peace and plenty. Hundred years today. Something special."

The girl turned to watch as the leading edge of the procession moved overhead, but she seemed unimpressed and quickly lost interest. Gazing down into the street, she followed the shadows of the parade crawling across the pavement far below.

"Lots of progress, know?" he encouraged. "New treaty, new trade laws . . . more metals, better technology, new drugs . . . and more freedom, too. . . ."

"Yo." She nodded. "More freedom. Free to work in Colony factories, free to build Colony machines, free to do Colony labor. . . . Freedom to be servants."

The cheering grew louder, and the boy looked to see the larger floats rising above the crowd, moving slowly overhead. The music reached a peak as streamers were launched over the rooftops, and the children cried out with surprise. The girl hesitated, then turned to look.

Someone was pointing to the first of the large floats as it came near, and soon the entire gathering was following its passage, observing its passenger with wonder.

"It's Cavernstone Blue!" someone yelled.

Straining his eyes to stare into the protective bubble at the prow of the float, the boy caught a glimpse of the alien within its murky green atmosphere.

"Hey!" he shouted. "It is!"

The girl turned to him, suddenly curious.

"What is?"

"Cavernstone Blue." The boy smiled. "That's its name in English, anyway. First Colonist to fly solo from Homeworld to Earth! Just in time for Year One Hundred, too!"

Looking up again, the girl glared at the thing within its weapon-proof shield. When it raised itself on four stalks and shook its topmost stems, it seemed to be waving to the crowd.

"Colonists not all bad," the boy argued. "Cleaned up the air and water, solved the population problem, gave us weather control, solar power, space travel . . ." The girl began to laugh, a sad, hollow laugh that startled him.

"Cleaned up the world by suppressing technology. Reduced population by killing resisters. Gave us nothing but demands. Can humans control weather, use solar power, travel in space? Can't even leave this city without permission, know?"

"But there's so much to learn," he countered. "Colonist technology is—"

"—is Colonist technology. Think humans will ever build starships? Powerpods? Warp-radio? Laser-cannon? Think Colonists will teach us that? All Colonists teach is slavery."

The boy said nothing, troubled to find his opinions so easily dismissed.

"Wanted to write something yesterday," the girl said quietly, almost talking to herself. "Wanted to see my thoughts on paper. . . . Ha! No one has paper! Aren't any trees! Aren't any plants or animals! Colonists changed the whole world to build Colony! Even took away our moon!"

Unable to answer, the boy gazed up at the flying procession that now filled half the sky. Directly overhead, children riding the larger floats were waving and throwing sparklers down to the rooftops. The crowd cheered and waved back, tossing lightning flares to show their approval, and everyone everywhere was smiling . . . except the girl.

"Not fair," she sighed. "Our planet, know?"

Trying to ignore her, he closed his eyes and let the spirit of celebration grow inside him again. Everything she told him was true. He knew it. But there was nothing to be done about it. Nothing to do at all, except party. Life was just one long search for reasons to party. Feeling better, he turned to face the girl with renewed enthusiasm, anxious to share his thoughts.

Then he realized she was gone.

He glanced about the rooftop quickly with a growing sense of panic, knowing he would not find her there. Reaching into his pocket he grabbed a tab of micro and swallowed it quickly. His hands were shaking as he moved away from the precipice, determined not to look down.

The drug kicked in quickly, and in moments he was calm again.

Soon he decided there was no reason for concern.

There was only a reason to party.

There was a parade.

YEAR ONE THOUSAND

It was a glorious day on Colony K'Mirra.

Rose-colored clouds drifted lazily across a burgundy sky, and the small amber suns turned slowly in their closely coupled dance as they wandered nearer to zenith. The winds were from the west, calm and cool, scented with sea-borne flowers and ocean spray, and only the soft, lulling songs of predatory birds disturbed the morning's peace.

Moving like a wraith above the landscape, a small boy with long, dark hair rode a silent airsled over the meadows to the very edge of native territory. With great skill and care the rider steadily slowed the floating disc, until the vehicle was finally brought to rest on a large patch of orange moss not far from the border. A few steps away, the vibrant colors of the meadowmoss ended abruptly, and beyond lay only dark-gray, sterile ground, creating a line that marked with perfect accuracy the outermost perimeter of Colony, where nothing native was permitted to grow.

Leaving the airsled unguarded, the boy slipped a small backpack onto his shoulders, prepared to walk the remaining distance. He paused before crossing the deadline, then marched rapidly onto the barren plain of ash and dust, leaving a long trail of small gray clouds in his wake.

The core structure rose from the devastated land like a great frozen froth, a vast network of interlocking domes filled with the murky green air of Homeworld, and at the base of the nearest dome, a gently tiered abutment formed a curving stairway of wide metal steps.

When he finally reached the structure's edge, the boy checked the chronometer on his wrist, then ascended the stairs quickly, stepping up onto a wide ledge that circled the entire complex. A single portal opened in the side of the structure, and the youth entered without hesitation, moving through a dark corridor to a transparent, bubblelike chamber within the dome's interior.

The lights of the reception area grew brighter as the visitor entered, and the voice of the Colony regent was heard on the speech simulator almost at once.

"You have not been summoned."

The boy waited, standing alone inside a small pocket of native air, gazing into the thick, green, alien atmosphere that surrounded him. After a long silence he saw the tall, bushy figure of the regent begin to take shape in the mist, growing larger and larger as it moved across the dome, until it stood beside the transparent airlock, towering over the human occupant.

"Respond."

"Something happened."

The regent leaned forward, its optical fronds focused on the youth, studying his face, his posture, but there was nothing about his appearance that seemed unusual.

"Explain."

The boy paused, then spoke in a strangely solemn tone.

"I have to go home."

The Colonist shook its petals in confusion. "That response is inadequate."

"True," the human sighed.

"You were assigned to assist the Colony engineer. Explain your presence here."

"Demolition was scheduled today."

The regent consulted its total recall to confirm the information. "A scaled tectonic macroblast will occur at Site Two within—"

"Demolition cannot occur as planned."

Long stems whipped the gloomy air in a show of displeasure. "Explain!"

"Still furballs on the island."

The Colonist appeared to relax as it lowered itself onto eight stalks.

"The animal life forms you term 'furballs' have been rated sentient at the same level of perception as humans. Evacuation instructions were issued on the broadcast networks in all native languages—"

"Some furballs understand, but still refuse to leave."

"Then those creatures that remain will be destroyed."

"Detonation could be postponed—"

"Delay is impractical," the regent countered. Then its manner turned skeptical. "Explain your concerns in this matter. You were employed on Earthlike worlds before. You terminated many life forms in the service of Colony. Perhaps your reluctance grows from their similarity to humans."

"Furballs?" the boy objected. "Look more like otters than people."

"They are animal. You are animal. Consider how this affects your judgment."

"Well . . ." The human bowed his head. "Suppose so."

The Colonist twirled its stamen in a show of satisfaction. "It is well you admit it."

"Their eyes," the boy explained. "Like human eyes . . ."

"Such emotional responses are common among animals. Perhaps you should be reassigned."

"Please, try to understand," the youth replied, his voice weak and tired. "I have to go home."

"Permission to return to the Colony of origin," the regent answered, "is not a valid request."

The boy glanced up, his young face strangely aged.

"Know what today is?"

The Colonist remained silent, uncertain, but the human went on without waiting for reply.

"New Year's Day," he announced, "Year One Thousand."

The regent checked its memory. "You refer to time scales and customs associated with your planet of origin; an anniversary celebrating colonization."

"Thousand years today." The boy nodded. "Calculated the date myself."

"Explain the relevance."

"Met a girl on New Year's Day in the year One Hundred." As he spoke, his voice began to fade. "Tried to forget her. Such a long time ago, but I still remember the way she looked, the sound of her voice . . ."

"There is no apparent relevance."

"Her eyes," the boy sighed. "Never will forget her eyes."

"Be warned. Your response is perceived as irrational. Failure to provide the proper response to—"

"Don't know the proper response!" the youth shouted. "Don't know how to make you understand! Can't do this anymore! I have to go home!"

"You are from Colony Earth," the Regent reminded him.

"Yo."

"That Colony is fully established. The entire planet was terraformed to Homeworld standard. You would find the air unbreathable, the temperature unbearable; you could not even survive without life support. The world you knew no longer exists."

The boy lowered his eyes and spoke in a whisper. "I know."

"You are a Colonial subject. You serve on the planet you are assigned. There is nowhere else for you to go."

The boy checked his chronometer again. Then he slipped the backpack from his shoulders and removed a small black cylinder.

"This is yours," he said. "Came to give it back."

The regent recognized the device at once, and the speech simulator conveyed a sense of alarm. "A fusion cap!"

"Took it from Site Two this morning."

"Site . . . Two . . ." the regent said, rigid with fear.

"Had to plant the engineer to get it."

There was unmistakable terror in the artificial voice. "Irrational!! Irrational!! Detonation imminent!!"

"Tried to explain," the boy said. "I have to go home."

He held the warhead gently in his palms, watching the timer count down the last few digits.

"And I'm taking you with me."

BOOK CHARGING CARD

Accession No. _____ Call No. _____

Author _____

Title _____

Date	Borrower's Name	Date Returned